Effective Leadership Skills in Compliance: CCO 3.0 and Beyond

By

Thomas Fox

Table of Contents

Author's Note

As always this book is the work of several people. My wife Michele Rudland continues to inspire and help me thought the daily slogging of writing. Gini Deitrich, who I am lucky to call a friend and mentor, suggested this book to me. Also thanks to Matt Kelly for co-editing the book along with my wife.

Introduction

Over the past few years I have tried to provide the compliance practitioner with solid information that can be used to implement, review and enhance a US Foreign Corrupt Practices Act (FCPA) or UK Bribery Act based compliance program. I have written several books that provide the compliance practitioner with information that can be used for the nuts and bolts of compliance with a goal of providing the specifics of best practices for an anti-corruption/anti-bribery compliance program.

This book moves beyond the technical aspects that a Chief Compliance Officer (CCO) or compliance professional must master to have success in the field of compliance. In this book I aim to provide solid guidance about the non-legal, non-technical skills a CCO needs to move past CCO 2.0 to CCO 3.0 and beyond. This is the landscape where the truly outstanding compliance professional will move to make compliance a part of the everyday DNA in the manner in which a company does business.

Just as the understanding of anti-corruption and corresponding compliance programs have evolved, the CCO and compliance practitioner position will continue to evolve. This book provides you with the tactics and strategy to advance your own professional skills so that you will become one of the most important components of any business moving forward. For failure to move compliance into the very fabric of your organization, whether you manufacture cars in Germany, are a large multi-national retailer, extract minerals around the globe or simply do business in China, puts your company's reputation at risk in a way that cannot be measured or even foretold.

PART I - COMMUNICATION SKILLS

1. A Remarkable Compliance Experience

Jerod Morris is the Vice President (VP) of Marketing of Rainmaker Digital. He talks about the four elements of a great podcast listener experience. I find them to be an excellent format for any Chief Compliance Officer (CCO) or compliance practitioner to think through when trying to communicate the message of compliance or the specifics of your compliance program to your employee listeners. It is yet another way that the tools of social media can be adopted and adapted by CCO's or compliance practitioners to further communicate compliance into an organization. As Morris explains it, "You really are trying to create an experience for an audience. Take people on a journey, and I think the four essential elements really break down the components of what it takes to do that." His four elements are (1) Authenticity, (2) Usefulness, (3) Sustainability, and (4) Profitability.

A. Authenticity

Authenticity is the first of the four essential elements. Morris explained, "authenticity really boils down to knowing yourself, knowing your audience, and then understanding the intersection between the two." He went on to provide the following example, that "to create an authentic connection with anybody, first you have to know what you bring to the table. What knowledge, what experience you have, what your passions are, but I think sometimes people really mistake authenticity and transparency, and they think that being transparent and just putting anything out there is going to create a connection, but that's not true." As a CCO or compliance practitioner, you need to be able to share your passion for compliance and integrate it fully into the fabric of your organization.

B. Usefulness

This means the information you are presenting has value to your audience. Morris said this element has paths to audience use, are you there to: (a) entertain, (b) educate, or (3) inspire? Why is your audience listening to your presentation? The best podcasts, like the best presentations, combine elements of all three. You are certainly there to educate about compliance and if you can present it in an entertaining way, your employee base may be more inclined to listen and even participate. Yet if you can also add an inspirational component this could bring you the highest listener experience. Morris ended his thoughts on this element with, "People are coming to us to learn about the craft of podcasting, and so we've got to make sure that yes, we're going to do all three of the elements if we can, we've got to understand the number one thing people are coming to us for and make sure we give them that above all else."

The subparts are not in a vacuum or even two of the three should not be taken in a vacuum. So even if you inspire with your message, you need to have an educational component that your employees can take away and use in the business going forward. However if you cannot entertain them enough, they may have turned off from listening before you can even get to the educational lesson.

C. Sustainability

For the podcast and greater social media world, this means "show up, show up reliably, and show up reliably over time, because you can be building an authentic connection, and it can be useful, but if you're only there every now and then, if people expect you to be there and you're not there, or, heaven forbid, if you just don't even start in the first place, you can't really create anything remarkable." For the CCO or compliance practitioner I think this starts with being available and making a personal connection. Obviously this means getting out of the corporate office and into the field to meet your employee base. Since any Foreign Corrupt Practices Act (FCPA) compliance program will deal with foreign government officials and business outside the US, this means getting out into the international world.

But it also means more than simply creating a personal connection. While you can use these personal connections to help you communicate, you also need to keep your audience base abreast of any changes that may be relevant to them or could be used as good teaching points going forward. You could put on podcast or other training when new enforcement actions come out to highlight the lessons learned about the bribery schemes that got a company into FCPA hot water. You must sustain your momentum going forward.

D. Profitability

Most people think that this element relates strictly to monetary gain. However, even in the podcast and greater social media world, profitability is broader than such a facile analysis. Morris said, "It involves the experience. It involves us getting more out of the experience than we're putting into it, intrinsically, and in the same way, our audience is getting more out of the experience. All of those together, authenticity, usefulness, sustainability, profitability, they converge to create a remarkable audience experience. Whether it's person, you're planning an event, whether it's a party that you're having at your house, or whether it's a podcast that you're trying to create an experience over time."

These elements all come together in the final concept, which for his podcast training is the Unique Show Positioning (USP). Morris explained, "Unique show positioning is basically what makes you different, I think, especially in anything that involves content, and that involves content online. There are so many options now for people, and really it's not just with online content." However the other key is your audience and its expectations. Morris said, "The unique show position is really understanding the audience that you're going for, understanding the other options that they have, and making sure that you uniquely position yourself to stand out to get the attention in the first place. That way the audience has a chance to experience you and then judge you based on your merit. If there's nothing unique about you, if you're not positioned in a different way, then it's going to be very hard for you to get the attention in the first place."

For the CCO or compliance practitioner, the USP is a critical element in communicating the message of compliance. There is so much internal training and communications to employees that many messages can get lost. Overlay the email traffic and that most folks out there have a day job to try and do business and you begin to see part of the problem. Morris and his message from the world of podcasting and social media suggested doing something different to get the attention of your employee base. Provide compliance related information in a manner that will grab their attention. Use the social media tools available to you. Why not bring subject matter experts (SME's) on the FCPA to record podcasts and make them available internally? It certainly might be an interesting way to make education about compliance attention grabbing for your employees.

Morris' four elements of a remarkable listener experience can be used in any format to think through your compliance related communications. Morris provides you with a way to ruminate through the delivery of compliance information so that it will not be overlooked.

2. CCO as Compliance Project Sponsor

One of the skills you may be called upon as a CCO or compliance practitioner is the initiation, integration or enhancement of a FCPA compliance solution into an organization. Most assuredly, one of thing that is not taught in law school or in any compliance course is project management. As CCO, you may either lead such a project on a day-to-day basis or you may take the role of project sponsor, while delegating the day-to-day running of the project to a compliance practitioner in your group.

An article entitled *"How Executive Sponsors Influence Project Success"*, by Timothy J. Kloppenborg and Debbie Tesch, noted, "The role of a project sponsor is often overlooked. But for every stage of a project, there are key executive sponsor behaviors that can make the difference between success and failure." I found their article has some excellent tips for the CCO or compliance practitioner who may be facing such a task. The authors break the project life cycle stage into four stages: (1) Initiating Stage; (2) Planning Stage; (3) Executing Stage; and (4) Closing Stage.

A. Initiating Stage

In this stage there are three key activities that a sponsor should pursue. First, the sponsor needs to set the performance standards. This "can be accomplished in the project charter by stating goals about the project's strategic value and how it will be measured." But beyond the written details there must be a "clear understanding of expectations about performance" of which dialogue is critical. Second, the project sponsor must mentor the project manager, whose key responsibility is to explain, "how the project fits into the big picture, defining the performance standards and helping the project manager set priorities." Finally, the project manager must establish the project priorities, with the "most compelling" questions being "what needs to happen first and how should conflicts by settled?"

B. Planning Stage

Here the authors believe that there are two critical project sponsor behaviors. The first is to "ensure planning" activities are completed by providing "leadership so that the project manager and team can set goals that align with the vision and broader organizational goals. The second is to "develop productive relationships with stakeholders". This means frequent meetings and communications. Interestingly, the project sponsor should not only see that "needs are identified and understood" but also make "sure that stakeholders' emotional concerns are given adequate consideration." Admittedly this is not something lawyers do particularly well but it is mandatory for the CCO or compliance professional.

C. Executing Stage

In the Executing Stage the authors identify three elements. First the project sponsor must "ensure adequate and effective communication." This means that regular communications must occur as the project progresses "to make sure that expectations are met." However this may require the project sponsor to "stand ready to manage the organizational politics with internal and external stakeholders." Second, a project sponsor must work to help "maintain relationships with stakeholders." This element helps facilitate the project manager and project team communications noted in the first element. Here the project sponsor should be "open to direct feedback from team members" to ensure that expectations are met. Finally, the project sponsor should work to "ensure quality" by practicing "appropriate decision-making methods and work to resolve issues fairly."

D. Closing Stage

Finally, in the Closing Stage the authors write that there are two elements that project sponsors should emphasize. The first is to "identify and capture lessons learned." They should be properly "categorized, stored and distributed in such a manner that future project teams will be able to understand and capitalize on". The second element is to "ensure that capabilities and benefits are realized." Capabilities, the authors suggest, "could include employees becoming more committed and more capable". Further, that processes are "more effective and efficient." Benefits relate to "verifying that the deliverables that were specified at the beginning were actually provided, work correctly and satisfy customer needs."

To the extent they know much about project management, most CCOs or compliance practitioners are aware of the "iron triangle" of factors to determine a project success. The authors define these as "cost, schedule and performance." But the authors' research has led them to conclude that for a project to be a success it must meet an organization's expectations. The next evaluative point is did the project come in on time, within budget and to the project's specifications? Finally, did the project succeed in bringing its touted positive benefits to the organization?

By using the steps the authors have outlined, a CCO can think through the organization and ongoing performance of a project to set it up for success. Equally important for the CCO, if the project management has been delegated to compliance team members or with other disciplines inside your organization, such as Legal, Internal Audit, IT or Human Resources; the continued involvement of a CCO as the project sponsor can be key component. The authors posit, "for every project stage, there are success factors that project sponsors should consider" and that a CCO must engage in an ongoing and continual dialogue with the project manager. Finally, key lessons learned should be captured and used down the road to help facilitate other projects or issues as applicable.

3. Why Compliance Should Widen its Circle

To be successful a CCO or compliance practitioner must have a wide circle of not only influence but also a wide network to help respond to your company's needs. In a Financial Times (FT) article, entitled "*Interact with a wider circle and your ideas will take flight*", Herminia Ibarra wrote about the concept that through the widening of social media use by businesses they can garner greater information and influence.

Ibarra referred to University of Chicago sociologist Ron Burt, who "showed what matters about a social network, whether face-to-face or virtual, is neither its size nor the prominence of its contacts but the extent to which it provides exposure to people and ideas you do not already know. People whose networks span what he calls "structural holes" - meaning the gaps between groups of people - tend to be more innovative and successful. They get higher compensation, better performance evaluations and more promotions. This is because they are exposed to alternative ways of thinking and behaving and can then connect those novel elements to local needs."

She wrote about a study that demonstrated that the "highest ranking ideas came from managers who had contacts outside their most immediate work group." This is in contrast with most managers who only discuss ideas from a "close and compact circle of immediate colleagues" which generally restricts the development of ideas. She further notes that in most businesses, "widening circles are the exception, not the rule, because managers are busy with routine tasks and often operate in silos. It is not uncommon for even the most superbly trained executives to have networks that are literally redundant because most of their contacts also know each other."

Interestingly she pointed to the example of (Ret.) General Stanley McChrystal who had noted that adapting quickly in a fluid military environment, such as the wars in Iraq and Afghanistan, depended "not on better formal structures and procedures but on having people who can bridge the structural holes in any ecosystem." He further explained, "Lacking people who spanned the structural holes between the teams, valuable information would linger for days or even weeks before anyone would see it. Even when the new information reached the close-knit teams, they often failed to see its relevance because each interpreted it through their own disciplines, procedures, and cultures."

McChrystal "devised ways to integrate disparate units into a high-performing "team of teams". Swapping highly trained commandos and intelligence analysts - two groups with radically different training and world views - for six-month stints, and assigning previously neglected liaison officer roles to the highest performers, for example, created new connective tissue and improved the teams' collective intelligence."

Joel S. Marcus, the Chief Executive of Alexandria Real Estate Equities, profiled in a New York Times (NYT) article by Adam Bryant, entitled "*Taking the Ego Out of Leading*", also uses this technique. Marcus is a big fan of Google founder Eric Schmidt and his book "*How Google Works*". Marcus says you should strive to "hire smart, creative people and then not put them in boxes. Give them a lot of authority to do some great things and you're going to have great results." To help facilitate this strategy, Marcus does not use hierarchical reporting structures but rather works "to keep a flat, decentralized and cross-matrix reporting organization. We don't have an organizational chart; I actually ban org charts from being done because I don't believe in them."

Marcus works just as hard not to take fast and hard positions before he can interact with a wide group and hear out the facts. Bryant wrote, "If somebody says they want to do something, I don't normally say no. Instead, I'll say, "Well, tell me why." I may decide I'm against it, but I'm open to hearing you debate it. I never try to be dogmatic with a no answer. I always try to let the person win the day, and I'm egoless when making decisions. I never think, "Oh, I need to make that decision and I know I'm right." That was hard to learn for a while, but I've learned that lesson. I also always try to get people to have multiple solutions for a problem. I never want to be put into a corner or forced down one road. There ought to be alternative options that can be successful for us, and the key is to have strategic optionality."

4. Just Say No, the Power of No and Compliance

What is the first thing that you think of about Former First Lady Nancy Reagan? Right up there for me is her *Just Say No* campaign, which was her fight against not only drug abuse but also premarital sex in the 1980s. In a more modern era, CCOs fear being known as 'Dr. No' and compliance practitioners generally fear inhabiting the 'Land of No'. In practice this leads to a fear of having to say 'No'.

However sometimes you are called upon to do just that, channel your inner Nancy Reagan and *Just Say No*. Occasionally you must say 'No' to conduct which might violate your company's Code of Conduct or get your business in hot water for a violation of the FCPA, UK Bribery Act or other anti-corruption compliance law. Sometimes, as Chuck Duross once intoned, you may have to be *'The Alamo'* (not the slaughtered part, the line in the sand part). But sometimes you may want to say 'No' for yet another reason altogether; that being by saying 'No' you may actually be opening yourself up to other solutions.

I thought about this concept when I read an article in the FT Undercover Economist column, entitled *"The power of saying 'no'"*, by Tim Harford. Hartford who looked at saying 'No' from an economist's perspective referred to it as "hyperbolic discounting" which he, in part, defined as follows, "Adopt a rule that no new task can be deferred: if accepted, it must be the new priority. Last come, first served. The immediate consequence is that no project may be taken on unless it's worth dropping everything to work on it. This is, of course, absurd. Yet there is a bit of mad genius in it, if I do say so myself. Anyone who sticks to the "last come, first served" rule will find their task list bracingly brief and focused."

But there is another economic principle at play with the use of the word 'No'. Harford said, "It's the idea that everything has an opportunity cost. The opportunity cost of anything is whatever you had to give up to get it. Opportunity cost is one of those concepts in economics that seem simple but confuse everyone, including trained economists." Moreover by saying 'Yes' to one thing, we are by definition saying 'No' to something else. Harford believes that is something that should be considered if you do not say 'No'.

For Jan Farley, the CCO at Dresser-Rand, this concept is what he talks about when he says that you do not want to spread your compliance program too thin. Farley has said that you cannot stretch your compliance program so thin that you try and cover everything so that you miss the larger FCPA or UK Bribery Act risks that your company faces. For the CCO or compliance practitioner, this requires you to assess your risks and then work to remediate those risks going forward. But you cannot deliver the necessary resources to a risk unless it is properly evaluated. With such a protocol in place, you will then be in a position to not only say 'No' but to be able to articulate your reasons for doing so if a regulator comes knocking.

So if your company's sales model is to use third parties, that is probably your highest risk, then prioritize your time and compliance budget on managing that risk initially before you move on to other compliance risks. Conversely, if your sales model is to use employees, then put your time and effort into managing that risk through training and monitoring employees regarding their interactions with foreign officials. Do not spend your time, budget and energy on managing the risk of low to no-risk parties and issues. There is no substitute for carefully thinking through your company's risk profile.

Just Say No also relates to some ideas put forward in a NYT article entitled "*The Upside of Being Replaceable*", which profiled Kristin Muhlner, the Chief Executive Officer (CEO) of NewBrand Analytics, a provider of social media monitoring. One of Muhlner's early lessons in the corporate world was that everyone's replaceable. She said this was because large companies are run like armies where everyone is replaceable. However Muhlner found not only an upside to this concept but also comfort in it. She said, "The wonderful thing is that you cultivate this sense that you are not the center of the universe. If you leave, someone will replace you, the circle will close and it just doesn't matter. That lesson has been helpful because it is really easy, as you move up in your career, to think that you've got to be involved in everything." In other words, you do not have to know everything and by extension, you do not have to do everything. You can *Just Say No* sometimes.

Another key lesson Muhlner learned is patience. This can be with a person or a situation where you may need to "let things play out a bit. People often come to you and say "We've got to fix this now." And it's very rare that you have to act immediately. You have to have the patience to say, "I'm going to evaluate the situation and the individuals involved, and I might choose to act on this, and I might not choose to act on this right now.""

Muhlner's thoughts on how to advance culture were also insightful. She said that she has found employees want to feel connected. She said, "people just have this incredible thirst to be connected, and they need multiple reinforcing points of communication. I have to remind myself over and over not to assume that everyone knows something. I've started sending out an email once a week called "Where's Waldo?" The email is just to say where people are, like that our V.P. of sales is meeting with this company. It's amazing the reaction that it gets from people, because they feel like, wow, cool stuff's happening, and now I know why he's not responding to my email today. It helps." For the compliance practitioner, this clearly shows the power of creating and distributing short messages about compliance.

Harford's article and Muhlner's interview drove home a message that compliance practitioners may not usually embrace. Saying 'No' can sometimes be the right call when it comes to delivering your compliance resources to your compliance issues. While saying 'No' to high-risk business ventures may be a harder sell to CEO types, it may well be that Nancy Reagan's admonition to *Just Say No* can be more effective to deliver a better and more efficient compliance service to those who may need it the most.

5. Communicating Across Cultural Boundaries

One of the things most critical issues to a compliance function is breaking through a company's internal cultural boundaries. *"Getting to Si, Ja, Oui, Hai and Da; How to negotiate across cultures"*, by Erin Meyer, explained that the basic thesis is "managers often discover that perfectly rational deals fall apart when their [business] counterparts make what seem to be unreasonable demands or don't respect their commitments." She layed out a five-point solution that I have adapted for the CCO or compliance practitioner in communicating a compliance program across a multi-national organization.

Initially you look for as many cultural bridges as you can find because such a bridge can help you to understand what your international audience is communicating to you, in both verbal and non-verbal formats, during a wide variety of activities familiar to any compliance professional such as training, investigations or simple meetings where the compliance perspective must be articulated in any business setting. If you fail to have an understanding or even a person who can navigate these signs for you, here are five steps to help you out: (1) Adapt the way you express disagreement; (2) Know when to bottle it up and let it all pour out; (3) Learn how the other culture builds trust; (4) Avoid yes or no questions; and (5) Be careful about putting it in writing.

A. Adapt the way you express disagreement

Simply because someone disagrees with you, it is not a sign that the discussion is going poorly but that it is an invitation to engage in a lively talk. Meyer suggests the "key is to listen for verbal cues - specifically, what linguistics experts call "upgraders" and "downgraders." "Upgraders are words you might use to strengthen your disagreement, such as "totally," "completely," "absolutely." Downgraders - such as "partially," "a little bit," "maybe" - soften the disagreement. Russians, the French, Germans, Israelis, and the Dutch use a lot of upgraders with disagreement. Mexicans, Thai, the Japanese, Peruvians, and Ghanaians use a lot of downgraders. Try to understand upgraders and downgraders within their own cultural context."

B. Know when to bottle it up and let it all pour out

Obviously some cultures have very demonstrative ways of speaking and gesturing. However other cultures are not comfortable with such displays. You need to understand this key difference. Meyer writes, "So the second rule of international negotiations is to recognize what an emotional outpouring (whether yours or theirs) signifies in the culture you are negotiating with, and to adapt your reaction accordingly. Was it a bad sign that the Swedish negotiators sat calmly across the table from you, never entered into open debate, and showed little passion during the discussion? Not at all. But if you encountered the same behavior while negotiating in Israel, it might be a sign that the deal was about to die an early death.'

C. Learn how the other culture builds trust

Most Americans think that building trust in a business setting is gained by demonstrating your usefulness and competency in providing solid information. However this type of approach is not always the most effective across the globe. Meyer writes that there are two different approaches to building trust. They are cognitive and affective.

In the cognitive approach, you gain trust by "the confidence you feel in someone's accomplishments, skills and reliability." In short, you know your stuff and for the compliance practitioner there is usually not much higher a compliment. This type of trust is more valued by Americans, Germans, Australians and Brits. Meyer says this is the trust that comes from the head. Conversely, affective trust may be termed to come from the heart. But it is not simply emotive. It derives from "emotional closeness, empathy, or friendship." It means that you see each other on a personal level. Meyer believes that in the BRIC countries, Southeast Asia, trust of this type is not likely to be achieved until this type of connection can be made.

Some of the techniques you can employ to build trust are to, "Invest time in meals and drinks (or tea, karaoke, golf, whatever it may be), and don't talk about the deal during these activities. Let your guard down and show your human side, including your weaknesses. Demonstrate genuine interest in the other party and make a friend. Be patient: In China, for example, this type of bond may take a long time to build. Eventually, you won't have just a friend; you'll have a deal."

D. Avoid yes or no questions

This is something Americans have an innate amount of trouble getting our heads around. Most generally when we asks a direct question requiring a direct Yes-or-No answer; we expect that whichever the answer is, it will be adhered to going forward. In many other cultures that may not always be correct. In some cultures, it is rude to tell someone you respect and have trust for 'No' directly. So while they may say 'Yes', they may really mean 'No'. Conversely, even when the verbal response is a strong or even a multiple 'No' answer, it may simply mean that the party needs more time to respond.

This means you should try to avoid a simple Yes-or-No response, by asking a more open question that elicits additional information that will help provide the context for the answer. You should also watch body language and other signals more closely, "Even if something is affirmative, something may feel like no: an extra beat of silence, a strong sucking of breath" or a muttering. Be watchful and listen closely.

E. Be careful about putting it in writing

This last point may be the most difficult for the CCO and compliance practitioner, especially if you accept my mantra to Document, Document, and Document. In many cultures, even the follow up to a conversation with something in writing could well seem like a slap in the face, the lack of trust or even communicating that the listener did not comprehend what you were communicating. So you may need to do some additional amount of explanation around your written compliance documentation. Do not be dogmatic about it, but emphasize the need for written materials in the appropriate situation.

This may also present you with an opportunity during training or in other communications to use something other than plain texts. Consider pictorial examples of real situations. Given the paucity of bribery and corruption across the globe, there are plenty of examples you can draw on from a variety of settings.

Communications in compliance can be largely drawn around trust. For any compliance practitioner this is a key to working with your employee base across the globe. Implicit in building trust is that you get out of your home office and travel to your other office locations. While you can build cognitive trust through demonstrating your usefulness to an overseas business unit from your home office in America, you will never build affective trust sitting in the corporate office. Get out and about and meet your employees and build the trust that will allow a successful two-way communication.

6. Asking the Right Questions to Boost Your Compliance Program

Other than the skill of listening, asking questions is about as important to the compliance practitioner as any other that can be employed. Yet, equally critical is to ask the right question, which is an issue explored Brian Grazer and Charles Fishman in a Fast Company article, entitled "*The man of many questions*", a short piece about their upcoming book "*From a Curious Mind: The Secret to a Bigger Life*". I found their article to have some interesting insights for the CCO or compliance practitioner.

Grazer is a well-known and successful Hollywood director who has directed such movies as *Splash, A Beautiful Mind* and *Cinderella Man*. He believes that much of the success he has achieved is because he asks lots of questions. Indeed the authors write, "Questions are a great management tool." This is because "Asking questions elicits information" and it also "creates the space for people to raise issues they are worried about that a boss, or colleagues, may not know about." Further, by asking questions, you allow "people to tell a different story than the one you're expecting." Finally, and perhaps most significantly, they said, "Most important from my perspective, asking questions means people have to make their case for the way they want a decision to go."

Getting your employees to not simply talk to you but tell you the truth about how they feel or what they may be thinking is a key skill for any leader. As a CCO, you may find this particularly difficult in far-flung reaches of an international company, which is subject to the FCPA, UK Bribery Act or other anti-bribery/anti-corruption law. Whether you are performing a risk assessment or simply getting out of the corporate home office, you need to be able to engage employees across the globe and from a variety of cultures.

The authors suggest asking open-ended questions so you will not simply get a Yes/No answer. While the questions they discussed using related to Grazer's work in the movie business, I found them a good starting point for any CCO or compliance practitioner, "What are you focused on? Why are you focused on that? What are you worried about? What is your plan?" By asking these or other questions, such as "What are you hoping for? What are you expecting? What's the most important part of this for you?" as a leader, you can get much more engagement from the people with whom you work.

Say you are pursuing a high profit deal in a high-risk geographic area. You might want to sit down with the business unit person in charge of the project and ask him/her, what is your plan to sign this contract and execute it, consistent with your obligations within the company's FCPA compliance program? As the authors' note, "You're doing two things just by asking the questions: You're making it clear that she should have a plan, and you're making it clear that she is in charge of that plan. The question itself implies both the responsibility for the problem and the authority to come up with the solution." This type of approach allows those who so desire to step up, as "It's a simple quality of human nature that people prefer to choose to do things rather than be ordered to do them."

Equally important are the values you can transmit by asking questions. If you do have to fly to China or some other local office, you do not want to be seen as the US corporate executive coming to deliver some bad news or that costs need to be cut. By asking questions you can solicit ideas to help solve problems. The authors state, "Questions create both the authority in people to come up with ideas and take action and the responsibility for moving things forward. Questions create space for all kinds of ideas and the sparks to come up with those ideas. Most important, questions send a very clear message: We're willing to listen, even to ideas or suggestions or problems we weren't expecting." The authors dispel the notion that this is some Hollywood 'touchy-feely' management style by stating, "This isn't about being "warm' or "friendly"." Further showing curiosity by asking questions is not simply a "matter of style."

Near the end of their articles the authors make clear that the need to ask questions goes both up and down. They state, "As valuable as questions are when you're the boss, I think they are just as important in every other direction in the workplace. People should ask their bosses questions. I appreciate it when people ask me the same kind of open-ended questions that I so often ask." If employees feel comfortable enough to ask these questions, it can "allow a boss to be clear about things that the boss might think are clear, but which often aren't clear at all." They also rather interestingly observed that if a person asks a question, "then they almost always listen to the answer. People are more likely to consider a piece of advice, or a flat-out instruction, if they've asked for it in the first place."

You too can use Grazer's techniques to improve not only your leadership qualities in the compliance function but your organization's compliance function as well. The reason that asking questions is so much better than simply giving orders is that you have a vast talented workforce you can tap into it help you do business in compliance. But the *how* of doing a business process that is, or should be, burned into your company can be facilitated by possibilities that are out there in your employees' minds. To get at them you have to ask questions. The authors end their article with the following two lines that sums up what you need to create as a leader, the atmosphere where "nobody is afraid to ask a question. Nobody is afraid to answer a question."

7. Leadership is a Conversation

Ethical leadership is absolutely mandatory to have a successful anti-corruption compliance program, whether it is based upon the FCPA or the UK Bribery Act. Senior management must not only be committed to doing business in compliance with these laws but they must communicate these commitments down to the organization. But leadership is not limited to only to senior management within an organization. Tone at the Top begets Tone in the Middle; which begets Tone at the Bottom. At each rung there is the need for compliance leadership. In an article entitled "*Leadership is a Conversation*", authors Boris Groysberg and Michael Slind discuss how to improve employee engagement in today's "flatter, more networked organizations."

The authors posit that the issue of *how* leaders handle communications within their organizations is as important as the message. They believe that the process should be more dynamic and more nuanced and is a process that they term "conversational". Building on this concept they suggest a model of leadership that they call "organizational conversation" which resembles ordinary person-to-person conversations. They believe that this model has several advantages, including that it allows a large company to function like a small one and it can enable leaders to "retain or recapture some of the qualities...that enable start-ups to out-perform better established rivals." The authors have found four elements of organizational conversation that "reflect the essential attributes of an interpersonal conversation." They are: intimacy, interactivity, inclusion and intentionality.

A. Intimacy: Getting Close

You should focus on two skills: listening and authenticity, because physical proximity may not always be feasible but emotional or mental proximity is required.

As a corporate leader, a CCO should "step down from their corporate perches and then step up to the challenge of communicating personally and transparently with their people." This technique shifts the focus of change from a top-down hierarchical model to a "bottom-up exchange of ideas."

B. Interactivity: Promoting Dialogue

Interactivity should make a conversation open and more fluid. You can obtain this by talking with and not just talking to an employee. The purpose of interactivity builds upon the first prong of intimacy. The efforts to close the gap between employees will founder if both tools are not in place along with institutional support that gives employees the freedom and courage to speak up. The authors believe that social media can be a useful tool to help foster such interactivity, but care must be taken to ensure that managers do not simply use social media as another megaphone. The authors suggest that more than just social media is required and that something extra is needed and that is *social thinking*.

C. Inclusion: Expanding Employees Roles

Following on from intimacy is inclusion as intimacy should force a leader to get closer to employees while inclusion challenges the employee to play a greater role in the communication process. Inclusion expands on interactivity by enabling employees to put forward their ideas "rather than simply parrying the ideas that others present." Clearly this is the prong that brings employee engagement into the communication process by calling on employees to "generate the content that makes up a company story." Employees who become committed to a message can become the best brand ambassadors that a company can ever hope to have on its payroll.

D. Intentionality: Pursuing an Agenda

While the first three prongs of this model focus on opening up the flow of communication, intentionality is designed to bring a measure of closure to the process. The goal here is to have voices merge into a single vision of what the company's communication stands *for*. In other words, the conversation should reflect a "shared agenda that aligns with the company's strategic objectives" that will allow employees to "derive a strategically relevant action from the push and pull of discussion and debate." The role here for leaders is to "generate consent rather than commanding assent" for a strategic objective. The authors believe that this enables employees at the top, middle and bottom to "gain a big-picture view of where their company stands" on any issue which has gone through the process.

8. Tailoring Your Compliance Message

Another technique is to consider how to tailor your internal compliance message. It is based on an article in the September 2015 issue of Writer's Digest, entitled "*Think

Like a Nonfiction Editor - 5 Key Questions to Ask Yourself In Revising Your Article or Book", by Debbie Harmsen. She asks you to step back and consider how your editor will view your book or article. I have adapted her insights for the CCO or compliance practitioner.

A. Is your message tailored to the right audience?

It would seem to be a basic axiom that any compliance practitioner would write a message about compliance. Harmsen cautions that you need to not only "strike the right note" but also set the right tone. This may mean you adapt your compliance message differently for different groups of employees. It would seem self-evident that a message that resonates in the US may not resonate with the same force in China or some other far-flung geographic location outside the US.

B. Have you chosen the strongest possible structure?

Harmsen writes, "Structure is critical to *every* piece of writing. It's the framework that hold content together. It guides the reader along and, in doing so, subtly lets them know they can trust you... If your structure helps readers know where they're going and feel confident about the types of information and entertainment they'll get along the way, they're more likely to trust you and what you have to say." For the compliance practitioner they key is whether your message is consistent and cohesive. Make sure you do not send mixed signals.

C. Am I offering overall takeaways?

How many times have your heard the business folks say, *don't tell me the rules, tell me what I can and can't do.* Any communication you make as a compliance practitioner is made to convey information. So have you provided any useful information that the business team can put to use in their day-to-day operations? Harmsen ended with a great line that I think sums it up neatly, "A good gut check when you're revising your piece is to see if you executed your story in such a way that it lives up to your title/subtitle's promise." Does your message match up and provide a solid takeaway that the title promised?

D. Does each section or chapter have a clear purpose?

I often rewrite compliance policies and procedures that were drafted by lawyers in law firms who have never practiced law, let alone compliance, from an in-house perspective. Needless to say these policies and procedures read like lawyers wrote them for lawyers to read and digest. The businessperson trying to read the company policy and do the right thing has little to no chance in such scenarios. Harmsen's dictum to "look at each section of your article or each chapter of your book and note what purpose it serves to the overall piece. If it doesn't have one, it likely needs to be either revised or cut" translates precisely into communications from the compliance function. If language does not serve a purpose, make sure that it does in the final version. Finally, make sure that everything appears "in an order that flows logically and easily from one to the next".

E. Is my voice authoritative without being overbearing?

Harmsen nails her final section with the following, "Where is your ego in all of this? Are you like the guy who is trying too hard to impress his date?" The core of writing is like the core of compliance communications; it is about the content and not about you, the author. You certainly need to be competent in your communications around compliance but you need to also make sure your content is competent and at the end of the day that it is what your written, verbal or video compliance message is about.

9. How to Keep From Losing it All

One thing not often considered by a CCO is the collapse of your reputation or that of the compliance function in the workplace. This issue and some others rarely talked about were explored in the NYT article entitled *"Beware the Threats to a Positive Workplace"* which profiled Greg Schott, the CEO of MuleSoft. I was particularly interested in Schott's reply to the question about the lessons learned about culture along the way of his career path. His response was quite telling and one that I think CCOs or compliance practitioners should consider in all their actions going forward. Schott said, "I learned that it can take years to build a great culture and you can tear it down in very short order. It's like a building - you can spend years building a beautiful building and then it can just collapse."

Schott listed four reasons that he has seen reputations collapse suddenly. First is the "lack of communication, which can lead to a lack of trust. If people don't feel connected to the leadership and they don't feel like they understand where the company is headed, people will fill in the blanks, and often not with positive things." It is mandatory that any CCO or compliance practitioner communicates not only what they are doing when interacting with the business folks but also why they are doing it.

Second is the situation where "leadership that looks like they're out for themselves. People pick up on that when decisions are made that are not necessarily with everybody's best interest at heart. It's hard to put your finger on it, but it's an attitude." Such an attitude is obviously corrosive in any organization or discipline within an organization but none more so than in the compliance function. Never forget that without business there is no need for compliance and if there is one overhead function that must get out of the office and meet the troops in the field it is the compliance function.

Interestingly, Schott next identified factionalism as a problem. He said, "I've seen this in the tech world as companies grow quickly. There tends to be an old-timer group - the ones who have been around forever, which in technology is three to five years - and the new people who were brought on board later." For the compliance practitioner I would point to siloed employees as a critical gap that must be bridged.

Finally, and I would say most importantly, is fair treatment and fair process. Schott said, "If there's any kind of different treatment, like the folks who have been there since the beginning are treated as if they're the only ones that can really figure things out, or if the new ones are considered the saviors of the company, that sends a terrible signal. We're all here together to make it work." I often say that you must treat the employees in South America that same as your top salesmen in the US. The same holds true that if you provide lessor sanctions for certain conduct, you cannot come down like a ton of bricks on a similarly situated employee.

Schott also had some interesting thoughts on hiring which I found has insight for the compliance practitioner as well. Initially he noted, "we're looking for someone who's a good human. That is defined by high integrity, being a great team player, and they want to win as a company first, team second, individually third. The next thing we look for is people who are whip-smart. The third thing we look for is a clear track record of achievement." Coupling both high integrity with being a team player can be a powerful tool to help bring a culture of compliance and ethics to an organization.

Yet it was Schott's thoughts in another aspect of the hiring process that I believe can bring insight into who you are hiring and what their underlying values are going forward. He said, "I also work hard to understand the decisions they've made along the way, like why they left a certain job to take the next one. You learn all kinds of things from why they made those job transitions. I'll also ask what they've done that changed things for their organization as opposed to just doing the job that they were asked to do. What did they do that nobody asked them to do?" When a CCO or compliance practitioner is asked to help evaluate a new hire or promotion of an employee up to senior management, they can use Schott's insights to make similar inquiries.

PART II - INNOVATION IN COMPLIANCE

1. Project Execution in Compliance

Not many CCOs consider the discipline of project execution in compliance. However it can be a useful innovation as was explored by Adam Bryant when he profiled Mark Toro, Managing Partner and Chairman of North American Properties - Atlanta Ltd., in an article entitled *"Who Will Do What by When?"*. Toro is a very results-driven leader. Yet it is not the maniacal devotion to data analytics that he rewards. He believes in allowing his employees to commit to something and then follow through with the commitment. Toro said, "There are only two types of people in the world: people who do what they say they're going to do when they say they're going to do it, and people who don't do what they say they're going to do when they say they're going to do it." The key is that you ask for a commitment to do something, complete a task or an assignment and then there is accountability for that person.

Interestingly Toro suggests that being a *creator* is a way to get ahead in business. When asked about what he would tell college graduates, one of the things that will set you apart is to create. He stated, "Whether you're a writer, a painter, a real estate developer, create something from whole cloth and do not be an intermediary. If you create value, you will be rewarded well beyond anything you could do from being in a middleman role, which makes you beholden to those who truly create the value."

However, it does not end at that point. Baker Hughes Inc. CCO Jay Martin has said that the difference in mediocre and great is in the execution. Toro obviously agrees when he said, "The process of conception, planning and execution is also hard for most people. And it's the last part where people typically have trouble, because execution is about doing what you say you're going to do."

Finally, he noted a key component of any CCO or compliance practitioner position, to manage compliance projects. Any program, policy or procedure implementation or enhancement is a project. It will require conception, planning and execution. Toro observes, "My perspective now is that everybody's a project manager, no matter what business you're in, and everybody's a salesman. The people who can marry those two skill sets will always have an edge."

2. Design Thinking in Compliance

In many ways the migration from CCO 1.0 to 2.0 to 3.0 and beyond is more than simply about the technical aspects of a CCO to the internal and external delivery of a compliance solution by the compliance function. The Department of Justice (DOJ) and Securities and Exchange Commission (SEC) both have consistently articulated that a FCPA anti-corruption compliance program should be an evolving solution, dynamic not static. Compliance as a business solution to a legal issue and must also evolve to meet the ever-changing business dynamics of a progressively globalized marketplace and international enforcement of anti-bribery laws. To think that the drafters of the FCPA foresaw every business challenge that would appear over the intervening 35+ years belies the path of legal and commercial developments in that time frame.

In an article by Jon Kolko, entitled *"Design Thinking Comes of Age"*, he posited, "the approach, once used primarily in product design, is now infusing corporate culture." For the CCO or compliance practitioner this means recognizing you have customers, i.e. your employees, and third parties that may fall under your compliance program. All of these groups have a user experience in *doing compliance* that may be complex and interactive. As a CCO 3.0 or further, you will need to design a compliance infrastructure to the way people work so that *doing compliance* becomes burned into the DNA of a workforce.

The first component of design thinking is to focus on the users' experience with compliance. Kolko stated that designers need to focus on the "emotional experience" of the users; he explained that this concerns the "(... desires, aspirations, engagement, and experience) to describe products and users. Team members discuss the emotional resonance of a value proposition as much as they discuss utility and product requirements." For the compliance function, this could be centered on the touch points the employee base has with the compliance function and that this should be "designed around the users' needs rather internal operating efficiencies."

The next step is to create something design thinkers use called "design artifacts". While this is usually thought of as a physical item they can also be "spreadsheets, specifications, and other documents that have come to define the traditional organizational environment." Their use is critical because, "They add a fluid dimension to the exploration of complexity, allowing for nonlinear thought when tackling nonlinear problems." Whatever the compliance practitioner may use, Kolko said, "design models are tools for understanding. They present alternative ways of looking at a problem."

Subsequently you should "develop prototypes to explore potential solutions" by building and testing a part of your system from the users' perspective. Here the author quoted innovation expert Michael Schrage for the following, "Prototyping is probably the single most pragmatic behavior the innovative firm can practice." I think this is because "the act of prototyping can transform an idea into something truly valuable" through use, interaction and testing. Prototyping is a better way to communicate ideas and obtain feedback.

While it may initially sound antithetical to the CCO or compliance practitioner, a key component for design thinking is a tolerance for failure. I realize that initially it may appear you cannot have failure in your compliance program but when you consider that design thinking is an iterative process it becomes more palatable. Kolko quoted Greg Petroff, the CEO at GE software, about how this process works at GE, "GE is moving away from a model of exhaustive product requirements." Kolko added, "Teams learn what to do in the process of doing it, iterating, and pivoting."

However design thinkers must "exhibit thoughtful restraint" when moving forward so that they can have deliberate decisions about what processes should not do. This means that if a compliance process is too complicated or requires too many steps for the business unit employee to successfully navigate, you may need to pull it back. I like the manner in which Kolko ends this section by stating that sometimes you lead with "constrained focus."

Kolko ended his article by noting three challenges he sees in implementing design thinking, which I believe apply directly to the CCO or compliance practitioner. First is that there must be a willingness to accept more ambiguity, particularly in the immediate expectation, for a monetary return on investment. A more functional or better compliance system design may not immediately yield some type of cost savings but it may be baked into the overall compliance experience. Second, a company must be willing to embrace the risk that comes from transformation. There is no way to guarantee the outcome so the company leaders need to be willing to allow the compliance function to take some chances in directions not previously gone. Third is the resetting of expectations as design does not solve problems but rather "cuts through complexity" to deliver a better overall compliance experience. This in turn will make the company a better-run organization.

James de Vries, in an article entitled *"PepsiCo's Chief Design Officer on Creating an Organization Where Design Can Thrive"*, focused on PepsiCo's Chief Design Officer Mauro Porcini. Porcini believes there are three key elements to embed design thinking in an organization's culture. First, there must be "the right kind of design leaders" because the discipline is so broad it requires a broader horizon than many traditional finance or legal grounded corporate types possess. You need a leader with a "holistic vision who can manage all aspects of design in a very smart way." Second, there must not only be senior management buy-in but active sponsorship because of the inherent resistance to change in any organization. Finally, there must be "as many external endorsements as possible - from a variety of entities" to demonstrate to your organization you are moving in the right direction.

Adi Ignatius, in an article entitled *"How Indra Nooyi Turned Design Thinking Into Strategy"*, profiled the PepsiCo CEO who brought Porcini into the company and sponsored his work around design thinking. One of the things she talked about was the user experience for Pepsi customers. I thought about that concept in the context of a CCO or compliance practitioner. How often do we focus on the user experience in the compliance discipline? I think as we move towards CCO 3.0 and beyond, we will need to do so to help burn compliance into the fabric of an organization.

3. Overcoming Biases in Compliance

n an article entitled *"Outsmart Your Own Biases"*, authors Jack B. Soll, Katherine L. Milkman and John W. Payne provided some insights into how to think through compliance issues. While noting that using your instincts is something we all engage n and can use to our benefit, the authors believe, "It can be dangerous to rely too heavily on what experts call System 1 thinking - automatic judgments that stem from associations stored in memory - instead of logically working through information that's available."

The authors believe the problem is that "Cognitive biases muddy our decision making... and even when we try to use reason, our logic is often lazy or flawed." They cite the cause of this problem to be that "Instead of exploring risks and uncertainties, we seek closure - it's much easier. This narrows our thinking about what could happen in the future, what our goals are, and how we might achieve them." Finally, as a solution they suggest, "By knowing which biases tend to trip us up and using certain tricks and tools to outsmart them, we can broaden our thinking and make better choices."

The authors suggest that to "de-bias" your decisions, you must broaden your perspective on three fronts. These are (1) thinking about the future, rather than simply one objective; (2) thinking about objectives, rather than simply the circumstances in front of you; and (3) thinking about options, rather than thinking in isolation.

A. Thinking About the Future

This is more than simply hedging your bets. The authors believe that "Because most of us tend to be highly overconfident in our estimates, it's important to "nudge" ourselves to allow for risk and uncertainty." They suggest that you use the four following techniques:

1) Make three estimates. The author's state, "To improve your accuracy, work up at least three estimates - low, medium, and high - instead of just stating a range. People give wider ranges when they think about their low and high estimates separately, and coming up with three numbers prompts you to do that."

2) Think twice. They suggest that you should "make two forecasts and take the average" because they believe that "when people think more than once about a problem, they often come at it with a different perspective, adding valuable information. So tap your own inner crowd and allow time for reconsideration: Project an outcome, take a break (sleep on it if you can), and then come back and project another."

3) Use *premortems*. I found this exercise very interesting. The authors explained, "In a *premortem*, you imagine a future failure and then explain the

cause. This technique, also called prospective hindsight, helps you identify potential problems that ordinary foresight won't bring to mind."

4) Take an outside view. Here, "You need to complement this perspective with an outside view - one that considers what's happened with similar ventures and what advice you'd give someone else if you weren't involved in the endeavor."

B. Thinking About Objectives

The authors believe that too often, "people unwittingly limit themselves by allowing only a subset of worthy goals to guide them, simply because they're unaware of the full range of possibilities." You should generate objectives and you can work to sort through them as you progress because by "Articulating, documenting, and organizing your goals helps you see those paths clearly so that you can choose the one that makes the most sense in light of probable outcomes."

The authors suggest two steps that will help to ensure that you are "reaching high - and far - enough with your objectives." First is that you should seek the advice of others, however, you should "Outline objectives on your own before seeking advice so that you don't get "anchored" by what others say. And don't anchor your advisers by leading with what you already believe... If you are making a decision jointly with others, have people list their goals independently and then combine the lists." Second you should cycle through your objectives by tackling them one at a time because by "looking at objectives one by one rather than all at once helps people come up with more alternatives. Seeking a solution that checks off every single box is too difficult - it paralyzes the decision maker."

C. Thinking About Options

Here the authors believe you should have a "critical mass of options to make sound decisions, you also need to find strong contenders - at least two but ideally three to five." They note, "Unfortunately, people rarely consider more than one at a time. Managers tend to frame decisions as yes-or-no questions instead of generating alternatives." The authors also believe that corporate groupthink tends to avoid a loss rather than reaching for a win. To overcome this, they suggest two techniques.

First, perform a joint evaluation because evaluating options in isolation does not ensure the best outcome. They write, "A proven way to snap into joint evaluation mode is to consider what you'll be missing if you make a certain choice. That forces you to search for other possibilities... That simple shift to joint evaluation highlights what economists call the opportunity cost - what you give up when you pursue something else." Second, they propose you use the "vanishing-option test" which requires you to "Assume you can't choose any of the options you're weighing and ask, "What else could I do?" This question will trigger an exploration of alternatives... That might prompt you to consider investing in another region instead, making improvements in your current location, or giving the online store a major upgrade. If more than one idea looked promising, you might split the difference."

Why is all this important for the CCO or compliance practitioner? It is because we are presented with options that appear to be simply Go/No Go or even one-off decisions. A FCPA, UK Bribery Act or other anti-corruption program should require a variety of responses. Just as all risks are different, the management of risks can be handled differently. As a CCO or compliance practitioner you cannot be Dr. No living in the Land of No; you must be proactive to come up with solutions to help your business unit folks to not only do business in compliance with the relevant laws but to actually *do* business. Just as a writer is able to weave an intricate story line into the traditional mystery format, you, as the CCO or compliance practitioner, should be able come up with solutions to the compliance issues that you face.

4. Supply Chain as a Source of Compliance Innovation

A Supply Chain Management Review article by Jennifer Blackhurst, Pam Manhart and Emily Kohnke, entitled "*The Five Key Components for SUPPLY CHAIN*", asked "what does it take to create meaningful innovation across supply chain partners?" Their findings were "Our researchers identify five components that are common to the most successful supply chain innovation partnerships." The reason innovation in the Supply Chain (SC) is so important is that it is an area where companies cannot only affect costs but can move to gain a competitive advantage. To do so companies need to see their SC third parties as partners and not simply as entities to be squeezed for costs savings. By doing so, companies can use the SC in "not only new product development but also [in] process improvements".

I found their article resonated for the compliance professional as well. It is almost universally recognized that third parties are your highest FCPA risk. What if you could turn your SC from being considered a liability under the FCPA to an area that brings innovation to your compliance program? This is an area that not many compliance professionals have mined so I think the article is a useful starting point. The authors set out five keys to successful innovation spanning SC partners. They are: "(1) Don't Settle for the Status Quo; (2) Hit the Road in Order to Hit Your Metrics; (3) Send Prospectors Not Auditors; (4) Show Me Yours and I'll Show You Mine; and (5) Who's Running the Show?"

A. Don't Settle for the Status Quo

You should not settle for simply the status quo. Innovation does not always come from a customer or even an in-house compliance practitioner. Here the key characteristics were noted to be "cooperative, proactive and incremental". The authors emphasize that "you need to be leading the innovation change rather than catching up from behind." If a company in your SC can suggest a better method to do compliance, particularly through a technological solution, it may be something you should well consider.

B. Hit the Road in Order to Hit Your Metrics

To truly understand your compliance risk from all third parties you have to get out of the ivory tower and on the road. This is even truer when exploring innovation. You do not have hit the road with the "primary goal to be the inception point for innovation" but through such interactions, innovation can come about "organically". There is little downside for a compliance practitioner to go and visit a partner and have a "face-to-face meeting simply to get to know the partner better and more precisely identify that partner's needs."

C. Send Prospectors Not Auditors

While an audit clause is critical in any SC contract, both from a commercial and FCPA perspective, the authors believe that "Too often firms use supply chain managers as auditors when they are dealing with supply chain partners." The authors call these types of managers "innovation partners." Every third party should have a relationship manager, whether that third party is on the sales or SC side of the business. Moreover, the innovation partners are "able to see synergies where [business] partners can work together for the benefit of everyone involved."

D. Show Me Yours and I'll Show You Mine

Here the authors note, "Trust plays an extremely important role in supply chain innovation. Firms in successful innovations discussed a willingness to share resources and rewards and to develop their partners' capabilities." The authors believe, "Through the process of developing trust, firms understand their partner's strategic goals." I cannot think of a more applicable statement about FCPA compliance. Another way to consider this issue is that if your partner has trust in you and your compliance program, they could be more willing to work with you on the prevent and detect prongs of compliance regimes. Top down command structures may well be counter-productive.

E. Who's Running the Show?

I found this point particularly interesting as, for the authors, this prong means "who is doing what, but also what each firm is bringing to the relationship in terms of resources and capabilities." In the compliance regime it could well lead to your partner taking a greater role in managing compliance in a specific arena or down a certain set of vendors. Your local SC partner might be stronger in the local culture, which could allow it to lead to collaborations by other vendors in localized anti-corruption networks or roundtables to help move the ball forward for doing business in compliance with the FCPA or other anti-corruption laws such as the UK Bribery Act.

The authors ended by remarking, "we noticed that leveraging lean and process improvement was mentioned by virtually every firm." This is true in the area of process improvement, which is an essential nature of FCPA compliance. Another interesting insight from the authors was that utilization could increase through such innovation. Now imagine if you could increase your compliance process performance by considering innovations from your third parties? The authors conclude by stating that such innovation could lead to three "interesting outcomes 1) The trust and culture alignment is strengthened through the partnership innovation process leading to future innovations and improvement; 2) firms see what is needed in terms of characteristics in a partner firm so that they can propagate the success of prior innovations to additional partners; 3) by engaging supply chain partners as innovation partners, both sides reap rewards in a low cost, low risk, highly achievable manner." With some innovation you may be able to tap into a resource immediately available at your fingertips, your Supply Chain.

5. Disruption Innovation in Compliance

How does disruption innovation apply in the compliance function? I was intrigued about the possibilities when I read *"Disruptive Innovation?"* by Clayton M. Christensen, Michael E. Raynor and Rory McDonald, where they detailed three key elements of disruption theory, which I have adapted to the compliance context.

The first is that compliance is a process. While this may seem as about the most self-evident statement one can make, I have to report that I have been contacted by a company who wanted an 'off the shelf' compliance package. They wanted me to do a couple of interviews of senior management and then put in some canned software program so they could claim they had a compliance program.

This attitude demonstrates the continuing battle the DOJ and SEC face when communicating their expectations around compliance programs. Compliance programs should evolve as business risks change. Just as disruptive innovation tends to focus on process, your compliance program should focus on your overall business process to be successful.

The second key point is that Compliance 3.0 is very different from compliance programs of the past decade. As compliance programs mature and we see the structural changes brought about by the Compliance 2.0 model, it is evident that we have now moved on to Compliance 3.0 where compliance is put into the fabric of an organization. The compliance function is moving from a solutions shop, where all compliance functions are centered in the legal or compliance department, to a process function where the front line business teams can use technology and other tools to operationalize compliance. The authors point to new business models as disruptive and I think this concept translates into how compliance can be burned into the DNA of an organization rather than simply sitting in the corporate office in the US.

The third point is that not all disruptive innovations succeed. Here the authors write that disruption is only one step in both the creative and growth process. Throughout their article, they discuss Uber in the context of a disruptive business. However, Uber uses the smart phone platform, coupled with a superior rider experience as a part of its business model. For the compliance practitioner, I think the key concept is what SCCE President Roy Snell says are the three goals of any compliance program; to prevent, find and fix issues. You could also plug in here *McNulty's Maxims* (What did you do to prevent it? What did you do to detect it? What did you do after you found out about it?).

This is why any successful compliance program should have multiple levels of oversight built into it. If something does slip through, a level of oversight should be in place to review it and, hopefully, prevent it. Consider BHP Billiton's FCPA enforcement action. It involved gifts, travel and entertainment around the 2008 Beijing Olympics. The issue was not that foreign officials were feted at the event. The issue that got the company into trouble was that they did not perform proper oversight over their carefully crafted program. A similar issue was seen in the Lily FCPA enforcement action where an oversight committee approved charitable donations without any substantive review and distributor commission rates were approved outside the standard range without appropriate review.

Disruption innovation has come to the compliance arena. One of the best examples is Louis Sapirman, the CCO at Dun & Bradstreet, who has incorporated not only social media tools but also the concepts of two-way communications into his company's compliance program. Another that springs to mind is Scott Lane, Executive Chairman of the Red Flag Group, who was one of the first and certainly most consistent commentators on the use of your own company's data to facilitate a straight line of sight by a CCO or compliance practitioner into transactions needing more detailed reviews.

As many compliance practitioners are lawyers, we are naturally reticent to embrace such change, however I think we need to embrace the need for continued evolution of anti-corruption compliance going forward.

6. Chief Compliance Officer as Enterprise Leader

One of the areas that a CCO must master is looking beyond their own compliance department to the company as a whole. CCOs must not only lead their own compliance function but also lead with an enterprise wide perspective. Simply put, the nature of any CCO position is an enterprise wide role to *prevent, detect and remediate* any compliance issues before they become full-blown FCPA violations. Yet this enterprise wide mindset is something that any CCO or indeed compliance practitioner must develop.

This issue was explored in an article by Douglas A. Ready and M. Ellen Peebles, entitled "*Developing the Next Generation of Enterprise Leaders*", and is useful for taking the compliance practitioner from implementing their vision of a compliance department to learning to build with an enterprise perspective. The reason would seem obvious; compliance demands an integrated response across "functional, geographic and business unit boundaries."

It also seems that successful enterprise leaders are able to see "the importance of the micro and macro simultaneously". A successful CCO understands that no one size fits all in compliance. This is certainly magnified across an organization. The authors said, "their trust in their leaders and their peers enabled them to share successes and combat difficulties together." This is mandatory space for any CCO or compliance practitioner.

As CCO you should build a compliance vision, strategy and brand and then broker shared meaning across the company. You should build enthusiasm for the compliance program and combine this with a sense that everyone in the organization is responsible for compliance. You should build compliance department capabilities and teams to broker the talent and turn the knowhow into an integrated compliance function across the organization. You should build support for compliance values and principles and burn them into the company's DNA. Yet, even beyond the personal stakes of the CCO are the benefits to the overall organization of a CCO with an enterprise leader mindset. A compliance solution should be integrated across an organization so the business units can work together in a seamless fashion. Such an approach also brings more and great efficiencies.

The authors believe the key essence of an enterprise leader comes from combining ""two often incompatible roles" - those of a builder and broker." This means that any CCO must integrate their vision for compliance across an organization by integrating it "into the wider corporate vision, clarifying where the organization and where their teams can best contribute, both within and beyond unit, geographic and functional boundaries." The authors identified "six components of the mindset of successful enterprise leader."

1. **Heightened Sense of Place**. By absorbing a corporate culture, a CCO can use that sense of the company as a competitive advantage. Further, such persons can transmit that passion to others in the organization. In today's hyper-transparent world of reputational risk, a culture of compliance can be a business differentiator. Yet with all senior management leadership, it is what you do more than what you say.
2. **A Broad Sense of Context.** Here the authors intone that it is the integration of understanding the business of a company with all its various components. It is not simply the crossing of siloed boundaries but understanding the differences in business units, corporate functions and even geographic locations that can bring this broad sense of context.
3. **A Sharp Sense of Perspective.** Interestingly the authors believe this skill is having the ability to see the big picture but "also appreciate the pixels that make up the picture." CCOs need to learn from everyone in the organization,

which can open up exposure to different leadership styles, how such leadership styles work in various areas and with different constituencies. The CCO should use other learning tools such as coaching, mentoring and observation to see what really works.

4. **A Powerful Sense of Community.** The authors believe that high-potential talent employees are "drawn to peer networks which challenge and support them." The CCO should cultivate his or her own personal and professional network. Many companies have a Chairman's Group or President's Group to challenge such individuals. Any chance to participate in such an opportunity should be accepted.

5. **A Deep Sense of Purpose.** Passion. The authors believe that enterprise leaders are "exceptionally passionate about their careers and their companies." I would certainly hope that a CCO or compliance practitioner would have passion in this field. However the authors believe such passion can occur as a result of "reflection, introspection and ability to change as a leader." Moreover, "rather than influencing employees through individual speeches or stories, the everyday connections between" a CCO's sense of purpose and the compliance vision can work to "form an indelible impression" about the importance of compliance to an organization.

6. **An Abiding Sense of Resiliency.** The authors said that enterprise leaders need to have a next generation mindset; knowing where you came from is certainly important but enterprise leaders must be "fit for the future" and be committed to continuous improvement going forward. The authors made clear this is not "organizational agility" or even the ability to pick one's self up after a setback but rather the ability to "pivot to the future" even after a stumble.

By using these six components a CCO or compliance practitioner can bring greater corporate wide presence to the compliance function. Integrating these steps into an already forward and outward looking regime can give compliance the tools to make the *doing* of compliance second nature within an organization. For if you can make compliance a part of the business process it becomes second nature and a recognized part of any business transaction.

The authors ended their piece with a quote from Bill Carapezzi, Pfizer VP for Finance and Global Operations, who said, "As I learned to work in new way at Pfizer, I developed better relationships and learned how to mobilize my team for the greater good, which enabled me to deliver more value for the company, and I just felt better." This would seem to be a laudable goal for every CCO as well.

7. How to Drive Compliance into the DNA of Your Company

An article in the Financial Times (FT) On Management column by Andrew Hill, entitled "*How to set staff free without plunging them into chaos*", had some interesting insights for the CCO or compliance practitioner on how they could think through driving compliance into the DNA of an organization.

Hill's thesis was that, "Two big assumptions blight efforts to change how large organisations work. One is that you had best start from scratch if you wish to introduce such exotica as flatter structures, autonomous teams and customer-focused innovation. The other is that you will only succeed in changing everything after a crisis or a wacky revolution". Not only rejecting these thesis, Hill believes they are "misleading" and it leads senior management to conclude it is "Better to try something that seems uncontroversial and is self-servingly supported by a team of paid advisers - mega-merger, anybody? - even if it is fraught with greater cost and peril."

The above description often sounds like something facing the CCO or compliance practitioner. Many C-Suite types believe that a FCPA anti-corruption compliance program will be a completely new set of bureaucratic procedures that will significantly slow down a company's business response going forward. To counteract this mischaracterization, I often tell such senior management that a FCPA compliance program is not 100 paces past what they are currently doing; indeed it is not even 10 paces past what they are doing. It may be 3 paces past what they are doing if they have anything close to the minimum of financial reporting controls.

Hill detailed another approach he is observing from companies. He said, "the truth is some traditional-looking companies are already shaking up their approach without drama and with the help of - not at the expense of - enlightened managers. Basic changes include the switch from rigid five-year plans to adaptable rolling strategies; or the use of a military-style mission-command approach, where chiefs set a goal and allow frontline troops to work out how to reach it rather than dictating every step."

He cited to the thoughts of General Sir Richard Barrons, head of the UK's Joint Forces Command, who told him ""I don't think you can run a business or organisation as if the leader is some giant satnav, telling everyone where to go." Managers increasingly must act as enablers of a network, rather than central controllers." Hill provided business examples from Ericsson, which has given autonomy to engineers to produce enterprise software for telecom operators and Microsoft, which he said is working "in a way to put Google to shame".

When senior management realizes that there is a business solution to the legal issue of FCPA compliance; then it will free the organization to move beyond having teams of lawyers driving what should be a business response to the business issue of corruption.

While not paying bribes is simple, as in you simply do not pay them; building and *doing compliance* is not easy, not only does a company have to want to achieve compliance but it also has to work at it. It is the *doing* of compliance where the rubber hits the road. Hill ended his piece with some of the experiences of Paul Madden from Ericsson. Madden intones that you have to do the work in this type of business structure. He said that his teams have to work harder. Whereas "In the past, when two teams did not get on, managers would simply swap staff around. Now they must moderate a discussion between groups. "It used to take two minutes. Now it takes two hours, but the result is a million times better," says Mr Madden. To put it in old-fashioned terms: that is a return on investment any board should be able to back."

The same is true in compliance. You have to put the work in but once you do, you can put compliance into the company as part of your business process. Think about third party management. The first step is a business justification and the final step, after the contract is signed, is management of the relationship. Your business unit contact is charged with completing the Business Justification form and that contact is uniquely situated to help communicate your company's message of compliance to any third party relation to your company.

If your business function has become imbued with compliance they can do these steps as part of your internal controls and it will make your company a better-run organization. Moreover, if they are asking such commitments from third parties, most probably such a businessperson would in better position to stop or report any issue that could eventually turn into a compliance violation. It is really not surprising to find those committed to compliance with others will also do business in compliance themselves.

8. Integrating Compliance into the Fabric of Your Company

The integration of compliance into the fabric of any company is the ultimate goal of every CCO and compliance practitioner. The disconnect between the written anti-corruption compliance program and the *doing* of compliance is one of the chief forces which can lead to violations, conflicting messages and objectives within any organization. If a company can amalgamate compliance into its very fabric there is significant opportunity for both efficiency and value creation.

Wendy L. Tate, Diane Mollenkopf, Theodore Stank and Andrea Lago Da Silva explored this issue in an article entitled "*Integrating Supply and Demand*". Their starting point is appropriately with Peter Drucker who noted the disconnect between the sales and SC functions was one of the "great divides" in management. Unfortunately the same can often be said for compliance and business operations. Many companies are "still trying to play off three sheets of music - the financial plan, the marketing plan and the operations plan - with results that seldom end in three-part harmony." You can certainly slot compliance into this more than occasionally off-key harmony. The question is how can compliance integrate into these functions to become part of the overall business proposition?

The authors posit that companies with only a single initiative toward integration are doomed to failure. To me that sounds quite a bit like the difference in having a paper compliance program in place and actually *doing* compliance. The authors identified five steps used by successful companies to coalesce these functions together.

1. **Develop a relevant value focus.** Senior leaders must set a tome on creating value for the organization through compliance. But this means more than simply lip service, as achieving this goal typically requires developing cross-functional structures and installing dashboard metrics that keep the business focused on implementing cross-functional integration.
2. **Share knowledge across the organization.** Managers must work on building inter-functional collaboration within the company, building external collaboration with SC partners and adopting technology that facilitates collaboration. This means more than simply training. Compliance practitioners need to be able to provide day-to-day guidance on how to do business in compliance with the company's articulated standard.
3. **Allocate resources strategically.** Once the entire organization shares the same set of facts, the company can then begin to make more thoughtful analysis of where and where not to allocate resources based on which customers deserve priority. Executives in sales and marketing should meet with the CCO or compliance practitioners to make decisions about how to create and fulfill demand for the business. This is where a risk assessment can move to a proactive document that can be a road map to not only enhance the compliance program but to strategically allocate compliance resources in a more agile manner.
4. **Learn to walk the talk.** Executives at this stage make individuals accountable not just for their own compliance performance but for the overall compliance performance of the organization. This should empower business unit representatives to make decisions that maximize overall value and develop new education and training systems that encourage collaboration all within the context of *doing compliance*. Finally, develop new incentive systems that encourage employees to stay focused on how to provide sustainable value to the strategic use of compliance.
5. **Balance capacity and demand.** All of the work in stages 1 through 4 is just a prerequisite to the final goal: To make sure that the company's most important business interest needs can be satisfied profitably. This typically requires streamlining processes and then developing flexibility and fluid scheduling to meet variable demand.

The authors conclude their article by noting that all of this is "not a functional-level process or even a process that exclusively focuses on integration between functional processes. It's an organization-wide orientation that spans functional domains and company politics to provide a basis on which to effectively and efficiently run an entire business enterprise. Building that capability takes time and effort. Leaders need to create the right organizational climate for integration and establish goals and metrics that align functions to organizational goals that enable the entire organization to create relevant value for customers of choice."

To facilitate this integration, the authors present what they term as three key insights for managers. Once again, while the article is focused on supply and demand integration, I found their insights applicable to compliance integration as well. The first is that *integrated knowledge is needed to guide integrated decisions*. This means there must be collaboration across a wide range of constituencies and stakeholders. In addition to those groups within an organization, it also includes third parties in both sales and SC. Second; *pursuit of relevant values requires making choices*. This means that your decisions must be based on verifiable data, otherwise you simply have internal battles solely based on anecdotal evidence.

Finally, and perhaps most importantly, *excellence is not enough*. For the CCO or compliance practitioner it once again comes down to *doing compliance*. Daily compliance execution requires coordination between operations, demand generating and the compliance functions to deliver the required level of value to each transaction. This requires both flexibility and fluidity of process, "fostered by internal alignment across operational activities."

Ultimately, "Rules, work arrangements and incentives may all need to be revised to keep everyone focused on the success of the partnership."

PART III - INFLUENCE FOR THE CCO

1. Hitting the Ground Running - Your First 100 Days as a New CCO

Now imagine that you finally have been able to secure a new position as CCO. Every company believes that they are ethical and that they certainly do business ethically but what are some of the things that you can do in your first 100 days? Hopefully you will not be dropped into a dire corporate situation but the reality is that many new heads are judged on these mythical first 100 days.

An article in Compliance Insider magazine, entitled *"The First 90 Days in Compliance"*, references *"The First 90 Days"* by author Michael Watkins as a starting point to provide "systematic methods you can employ to both lessen the likelihood of failure and reach the break-even point faster."

A. Prepare Yourself

The key is to try and make a clear transition. The best situation is if you can take some time off to prepare yourself between your old and new positions. You should try and use this time to learn more about your new employer and supplement the information you were able to garner during the hiring process. If you cannot take time off, the article suggests studying every night to prepare for your new position. If you want to hit the ground running, you have to be ready to do so.

B. Accelerate Your Learning

You will be required to learn quite a bit on the job, very, very quickly. The article suggests some key areas for immediate inquiry, which include your new company's investigations and hotline issues; the internal audit documents relating to compliance; the annual reports for any notes about investigations or other SEC issues; and a general review to see what is happening in the industry to see if there are ongoing FCPA investigations or recent enforcement actions. Another suggestion is to meet up to 50 colleagues in your new company to "Interview them about the company's existing compliance" program. From these interviews, you can reach out to begin to build a network for further interviews.

C. Match Your Strategy to the Situation

Here the article advises that you need to first identify the highest compliance risks and then try to focus on the risks that are not being managed effectively. They note, "It is your role to quickly work out where the most risky practices are and which risks will have the biggest effect on the business...The part that is more challenging is managing risk while focusing on the areas that have the biggest business value. Business value can be measured in country value, profit or reputation. It can also be measured in reducing potential exposure in fines or prosecutions, or growing revenue and profits."

D. Secure Early Wins

You do not need to try and fix the company's compliance program in the first 100 days. But you do need to find a way "to identify opportunities to build both personal credibility and credibility for the compliance function as a whole." The article advocates taking the issue that seems to have the most "noise" and contributing towards resolving it. But some of your work may come with instituting good process, as "A large amount of early wins can be as simple as the new compliance team focusing on adding value, removing obfuscation and helping to grow the business, rather than being a roadblock."

E. Negotiate Success

One obvious area to aid with your success in the corporate world is to have a good relationship with your boss. The article recommends you have conversations around "expectations, working style, resources and your personal development." To facilitate these discussions the following points are posited:

- There is no value in trashing the existing compliance program.
- You need to drive the discussions with your boss.
- Your boss is looking for solutions, not problems.
- Your boss is not interested in running through your checklist of things to do.
- Make sure that you connect with the people that your boss values and admires, such as their mentor.
- Most importantly, set expectations.

F. Achieve Alignment

If you did not garner enough information through the hiring process, you must have a clear understanding of what compliance means at your new company and what your role will be. While you were hired for FCPA or other anti-bribery legislation compliance, does compliance means something broader in your new role?

G. Build Your Team

You will probably be called on to make some difficult personnel decisions in this area but ones that are absolutely necessary. As the article notes, "your ability to select the right people for the right positions is among the most important drivers of success during your transition and beyond. You also need to hold onto the right people. The focus for every solid manager is to focus on the best people and only those people - the rest should quickly be managed up or out." If compliance is seen as 'The Land of No' populated by one or more Dr. No characters, it is time to make a change and the sooner the better.

H. Create Coalitions

One of the biggest keys for any successful compliance program is the ability "to influence people outside your direct line of control. Supportive alliances, both internal and external, are necessary if you are to achieve your goals." You will need to try and identify those persons and develop relationships, then create coalitions with them. This means you will need to get out of the office and get overseas as quickly as possible. While your manager, be it the CEO or other, will probably want you in the office, you need to get out of your office and build relationships in the field.

I. Keep Your Balance

These first 100 days will be a time of very high stress. This may well be compounded by your travel schedule and working very long hours to try and fulfill the concepts discussed herein. The article advises, "The right advice-and-counsel network is an indispensable resource. Use your network of mentors, coaches and friends to discuss your part at the company and what you have been experiencing." The key is to use whatever resources are available to you during your first 100 days.

J. Accelerate Everyone

The gold standard for the first 100 days is the first term of President Franklin Roosevelt. You should take the key component of FDR's success to heart in your new role. Engage all of your "direct reports, bosses, and peers - accelerate their own transitions. The fact that you're in transition means they are too. The quicker you can get your new direct reports up to speed, the more you will help your own performance."

2. As a CCO, How Will You Manage?

After your first 100 days, how will you manage? Do you manage as a leader or do you manage as a manager? Herminia Ibarra explored this question in an article entitled *"When a leader is not a manager and other modern myths"*. It provided a useful manner for any CCO to consider when thinking about how to influence a culture of compliance. While most organizations and their employees succeed when they do what they think is the right thing to do; the role of a CCO or compliance practitioner can be seen from both perspectives.

Ibarra states, "It's hard to think of a business idea that has had more sticking power than the distinction between leadership and management. And, as with most simple but powerful notions, the dichotomy is part caricature, part resonant truth. We have come to use it as a shorthand to distinguish the noble from the slavish, the outstanding from the ordinary, the good from the bad." She quoted business scholar Warren Bennis for the following, "The manager is a copy; the leader is an original."

Yet even using this stereotypical dichotomy as somewhat of a straw man, Ibarra stated, "Archetypes persist because they convey valuable lessons, but they are myths nonetheless and it's instructive to trace this one back to its origins. It started with sociologist Max Weber, who distinguished between forms of authority. "Rational-legal authority" is impersonal, based on rules and hierarchical relations that limit personal discretion. "Charismatic authority" is personal, based on exceptional individual qualities, insight or accomplishments, which inspire followers."

She noted, "management and leadership as different kinds of work, not different kinds of people. Management aims to ensure efficiency through routine planning, organising and co-ordinating; leadership aims to create change by envisioning a better future, aligning those who can make it happen, or block it, and inspiring them to do it." She drew from retired Harvard Professor John Kotter who urged that companies "require a mix of both, the right dose depending on context: the more complexity - more products, geographies, units - the more management is needed; the more volatile the environment, the more leadership is required."

The greatest insight was "When managing, one works within one's sphere of formal authority; when leading, one influences and motivates outside and beyond, since many crucial stakeholders are external." This would seem to me to be an excellent description of at least two hats that any CCO or compliance practitioner must wear. As a leader, you must focus on long term thinking and planning. What is your 1, 3 or 5-year plan for your company's compliance program? Have you planned this out? How about committing it in writing? If you answered yes to all the above, have you presented it to the Audit Committee or the Board of Directors? If it is simply an aspirational document sitting on your desk, it is not moving the ball forward too much.

As a leader have you gone out and visited your troops in the field? How have you worked with the business unit managers to help them achieve their sales goals from the compliance perspective? As a CCO have you inspired any employees to #Dotherightthing, through the use of innovative social media techniques to spread the culture of compliance in your organization? As a leader in compliance you are only limited by your imagination and that is certainly one way you can lead, through imaginative innovation.

Yet there is another role for a CCO or compliance practitioner and that is managing. Mangers work through process. Much of any company's best practices compliance program is through process, such as internal controls. Compliance management should work through technology and other routines to create greater efficiencies around risk management.

If it is not clear that compliance is clearly a mix of both strategies; consider this from Ibarra's piece where she quoted Patrick Cescau, former Unilever Group Chief Executive and current InterContinental Hotels Group Chairman, who said, "It's putting the strategy into action, embedding it in the fabric of the organisation and making it happen that is hard. For that you also need managerial qualities." The compliance function must work to inspire and put the processes into place that allow prevention, detection and remediation if a violation occurs. Clearly there must be "rules and hierarchal relations that limit personal discretion" but at the end of the day, employees must want to do the right thing. As a CCO you need to be able to inspire, manage and lead employees with your vision of how compliance can be burned into the DNA of your organization.

3. Do Your Executives Have Skin in Compliance?

How can you incentivize senior management to operate your business in compliance? Gretchen Morgenson explored this inter-connectedness of compensation in the corporate world and in a compliance program in an article entitled "*Ways to Put the Boss's Skin In the Game*". Her piece dealt with a long-standing question about how to make senior executives more responsible for corporate malfeasance such as those based on the FCPA or UK Bribery Act. Morgenson said the issue was "Whenever a big corporation settles an enforcement matter with prosecutors, penalties levied in the case - and they can be enormous - are usually paid by the company's shareholders. Yet the people who actually did the deeds or oversaw the operations rarely so much as open their wallets."

She went on to explain that it is an economic phenomenon called "perverse incentive" which is one where "corporate executives are encouraged to take outsized risks because they can earn princely amounts from their actions. At the same time, they know that they rarely have to pay any fines or face other costly consequences from their actions." To help remedy this situation, the idea has come to the fore about senior executives putting some 'skin in the game'. Her article discussed three different sources for this initiative.

The first is a current proxy proposal in front of Citigroup shareholders that "would require that top executives at the company contribute a substantial portion of their compensation each year to a pool of money that would be available to pay penalties if legal violations were uncovered at the bank." Further, "To ensure that the money would be available for a long enough period - investigations into wrongdoing take years to develop - the proposal would require that the executives keep their pay in the pool for 10 years."

The second came from William Dudley, the President of the Federal Reserve Bank of New York, who made a similar suggestion in a speech he gave. His proscription involved a performance bond for the actions of bank executives. He said, "In the case of a large fine, the senior management and material risk takers would forfeit their performance bond. Not only would this deferred debt compensation discipline individual behavior and decision-making, but it would provide strong incentives for individuals to flag issues when problems develop."

Morgenson reported on a third approach articulated in a Greg Zipes article, entitled *"Ties that Bind: Codes of Conduct That Require Automatic Reductions to the Pay of Directors, Officers and Their Advisors for Failures of Corporate Governance"*. Zipes proposed the creation of a "contract to be signed by a company's top executives that could be enforced after a significant corporate governance failure. Executives would agree to pay back 25 percent of their gross compensation for the three years before the beginning of improprieties. The agreement would be in effect whether or not the executives knew about the misdeeds inside their company."

As you might guess, corporate leaders are somewhat less than thrilled at the prospect of being held accountable. Zipes was cited for the following, "Corporate executives are unlikely to sign such codes of conduct of their own volition." Indeed Citigroup went so far as to petition the SEC "for permission to exclude the policy from its 2015 shareholder proxy." But the SEC declined and at least their shareholders will have the chance to vote on the proposal.

In the compliance context, these types of proposals seem to me to be exactly the type of response that a company or its Board of Directors should want to put in place. Moreover, they all have the benefit of a business solution to a legal problem. In an interview for her piece, Morgenson quoted Zipes as noting, "This idea doesn't require regulation and its doesn't require new laws. Executives can sign the binding code of conduct or not, but the idea is that the marketplace would reward those who do." For those who might argue that senior executives cannot or should not be responsible for the nefarious actions of others, remember they readily take credit for "positive corporate activities in which they had little role or knew nothing about." Moreover, under Sarbanes-Oxley (SOX), corporate executives must make certain certifications about financial statements and reporting so there is currently some obligations along these lines.

Finally, perhaps shareholders will simply become tired of senior executives claiming they could not know what was happening in their businesses; have had their fill of hearing about some *rogue employee(s)* who went off the rails by engaging in bribery and corruption to obtain or retain business; and not accept that leaders should not be held responsible.

4. More Productive Meetings

When in the corporate world I often felt the bane of my existence was the requirement to attend not only endless meetings but also useless meetings; which about 99.9999% met both of these criteria. So how can you make your compliance meetings more productive? This issue was explored in an article in the Houston Business Journal (HBJ), entitled *"10 ways to make your next meeting more productive"* by Dana Manciagli.

Manciagli began her piece by noting that researchers from the London School of Economics and Harvard University found that business leaders "spend 60% of their time in meetings, and only 15% working alone." While this statistic alone is troubling enough, when you overlay that with the number of meetings where nothing is accomplished, it is clear to me you have a complete waste of time and resources. I do recognize that some companies have taken accomplishing nothing in meetings as a matter of corporate policy. General Motors (GM) took this to an art form in the well-documented *GM Nod*, which signified that there was agreement on an issue but that no one would actually do anything about it.

But for those who might want to actually accomplish something in a meeting, Manciagli pointed to Andrea Driessen whom she described as "chief boredom buster" at Seattle-based No More Bored Meetings. How is that for a moniker and company name? Manciagli related Driessen's top ten tips for developing, running and ultimately having a successful meeting.

A. Be a Know-it-all

Manciagli wrote that because it is "natural to disengage when meeting content isn't relevant. The most effective meeting hosts review all potential agenda segments to determine whether they apply to all attendees. If participants already know a particular content slice, then simply don't cover that segment for the broader audience. Or if you have vastly different levels of awareness in the room, divide people accordingly to ensure maximum relevance for all." Of course this means you will need to put some thought into your pre-meeting planning.

B. No Problem? No Meeting!

We have all been subjected to it, the *daily, weekly, monthly* meeting check-in to see how the project is progressing. But Manciagli said, "many of these less-than-productive meetings could be canceled or shortened if we identified the problem the meeting is intended to solve. And if we can't find an identifiable problem, then don't have the meeting." She concludes, "Sometimes, it's that simple."

C. Get Real

This is another pre-meeting planning point. Do you try to squeeze 13 action items for discussion and resolution into a 30-minute meeting? Conversely you do not need to book a 60-minute window to handle a couple of points. If you can handle a matter via email or need to go offline, do so.

D. Prioritize, Prioritize, Prioritize!

Like its related cousin, *Document, Document, and Document*, this phase should be more than simply a catchword. It should be an action item in your meeting planning process. Tackle your important issues first to "save time and solve your most pressing problem."

E. Play "Pass the Pad" To Avoid Late Arrivals

The biggest offender of this rule is, unfortunately, a lawyer. The reason is that in our eyes, we are the most important attendees. Yet not being able to start because someone is not present or having to repeat points is one of the worst problems there is around efficient meetings. Manciagli noted, "Meeting productivity suffers when people arrive late, and the punctual are penalized." Her solution is to require the latecomer to take notes in the meeting, writing "People learn quickly that they can either be on time, or become the dreaded note-taker if they are late. As host, you'll see positive behavior change with little effort on your part."

F. Be a Meeting Bouncer

Manciagli tactfully writes about that "common meeting malady: the tangent talker." I would perhaps less tactfully say there are way too many people who like to hear the sound of their own voices way too much. Manciagli suggested a little humor by "naming a tangent officer who monitors and records tangents for later. Use that parking lot! And you can lighten it up by using a toy police badge." Nothing like a little corporate shame to keep things moving along.

G. Make it Multi-Sensory

It is not simply millennials who respond to social media. Most people do better when they are visually engaged. Manciagli suggested using more than simply oral presentations, use other tools, including "Graphic illustration, in which someone draws out ideas in real time; Customer testimonials that emotionally inspire; Quizzes and games; Product demos; Surprise guests; Props that foster kinesthetic learning."

H. PPPPP

Everyone understands the Five P rule; aka *prior planning prevents poor performance*. As a meeting host, this means you must absolutely be prepared prior to the meeting. If there are technical issues, you should pass out that information prior to the meeting. Manciagli pointed out "the more skin we all have in the game, the more likely we are to own and be accountable to group outcomes."

I. Hire an 'Accountant'

Accountability. How many meetings have you attended where there was no accountability? Manciagli wrote "Most meetings lack built-in accountability structures." She gives the tangible hint to "ask everyone to record at least one goal related to the meeting that they'll commit to completing in the next week or month, and have them check in with one another. Teams gain measurable accountability, and you get recognized for generating stronger results tied to your meetings."

J. Remember: Humor is No Joke

Humor has a big use in meetings, "The power of humor - if used effectively within the meeting mix - is no laughing matter. Indeed, there is a strong business case to be made for laughing while learning." It can also lower the stress level in meetings, once again if used properly.

I am sure that you have your own horror stories of aimless, wandering meetings that go nowhere painfully slow. As a CCO or compliance practitioner, one of your most valuable items in a corporation is time. You can set an example about running an efficient and productive meeting and then lead your company down the path laid out in the article.

5. Empathy in Compliance

Can you empathize with those who work for you, around you and those you report to? While many leaders, particularly those who might be labeled the 'command and control' type seem to think that empathy is a negative; I think that it is an important habit for any CCO or compliance practitioner to not only practice but also master. Recently there were a couple of articles in the NYT that discussed this character trait and I found them useful to consider for the leadership toolkit of the CCO or compliance professional.

The first was by Daryl Cameron, Michael Inzlicht and William A. Cunningham, entitled *"Empathy is Actually a Choice"* and the second was by Adam Bryant, entitled *"Is Empathy on Your Résumé?"* where he profiled Stewart Butterfield, the co-founder and chief executive of Slack, a communication service for businesses. The first piece focused on research by the authors and the second was Bryant's weekly piece on business leadership.

The researchers noted, "While we concede the exercise of empathy is, in practice, often far too limited in scope, we dispute the idea that this shortcoming is inherent, a permanent flaw in the emotion itself...we believe that empathy is a choice that we make to extend ourselves to others. The "limits" to our empathy are merely apparent, and can change, sometimes drastically, depending on what we want to feel." The authors ended by stating, "Arguments against empathy rely on an outdated view of emotion as a capricious beast that needs to yield to sober reason. Yes, there are many situations in which empathy appears to be limited in its scope, but this is not a deficiency in the emotion itself. In our view, empathy is only as limited as we choose it to be."

Bryant's article on Butterfield and his leadership style brought these concepts home. Most interestingly, Butterfield began by self-disclosing, "I'm good at the leadership part. But I've always said that I'm a terrible manager. I'm not good at giving feedback. People are like horses - they can smell fear. If you have a lot of apprehension going into a difficult conversation, they'll pick up on that. And that's going to make them nervous, and then the whole conversation is more difficult."

Another insight on leadership was something as simple as meetings. Butterfield said that "if you're going to call a meeting, you're responsible for it, and you have to be clear what you want out of it. Have a synopsis and present well. At the same time, if you're going to attend a meeting, then you owe it your full attention. And if it's not worth your attention, then say so - but don't be a jerk about it - and leave the meeting." So more than simply taking responsibility for one's own time, he put out the empathy to allow you to consider how your agenda (or lack thereof) may have negative repercussions on others on your team or in your organization.

Another interesting insight from Butterfield was his thoughts on empathy as it related to leadership. This is a sought out trait for employees, as early as in the interview process. He said, "When we talk about the qualities we want in people, empathy is a big one. If you can empathize with people, then you can do a good job. If you have no ability to empathize, then it's difficult to give people feedback, and it's difficult to help people improve. Everything becomes harder."

Similar to his examples around meetings, Butterfield believes that empathy can express itself as courtesy. He said, "One way that empathy manifests itself is courtesy. Respecting people's time is important. Don't let your colleagues down; if you say you're going to do something, do it. A lot of the standard traits that you would look for in any kind of organization come down to courteousness. It's not just about having a veneer of politeness, but actually trying to anticipate someone else's needs and meeting them in advance."

For the CCO or compliance practitioner, Butterfield pointed out specific areas where the trait of empathy can yield great respect for you and your position in any corporation. People rarely think of courtesy and respect as leadership skills but if you can bring these to bear in your compliance practice, you can garner greater influence as not only someone who cares but someone who cares and gets things accomplished. For any corporate disciple which relies on influence to succeed these simple tools can go a long way to providing to you a wider manner to impact corporate culture, become a trusted partner and be a part of any significant business conversation earlier rather than later in the game.

6. Managing Talent

In a FT article entitled *"Game of talents: management lessons from top football coaches"*, Mike Forde and Simon Kuper wrote about how "football [soccer for us Yanks] coaches grapple with egos, tantrums and rivalry. Business could learn a lot from them." This is because talent management is a key component of any successful organization and none more so than on a team where "Football managers are, above all, talent managers." It provides some interesting insights for the CCO or compliance practitioner whom I believe could be helpful when dealing with large egos found in any business organization.

1. **Big talent usually comes with a big ego.** Accept it. I grew up professionally in the private practice world of a law firm where big egos not only existed but also thrived and were cultivated. This is not always true in the corporate world. The authors believe that "managing difficult people is the best test of a good manager."

2. **Look for big egos that have 'gotten over themselves'.** At some point we all grow up. In the business world, just as in sports, "some players underperform early in their careers because they are immature." Maturity can lead players to "accept their limits and become coachable."

3. **Single out and praise those who make sacrifices for the organization.** Reward those who might be willing to make a personal sacrifice. If you do, your behavior as a leader will be noticed and others in the business may well do the same.

4. **The manager shouldn't aspire to dominate the talent.** In soccer "Talent wins matches...Successful managers accept this. They don't try to emphasise their leadership by dominating talent." As a CCO, you should not only work to help the business folks succeed but let them take the glory if a big deal is closed.

5. **Ask talent for advice - but only for advice.** While it seems self-evident, it always bears repeating if you take someone's advice to craft a solution, that person will then be personally invested in the success of that solution. The authors quoted David Brailsford, general manager of Team Sky, for the following, "We all perform better if we have a degree of ownership of what we do."

6. **The manager's job isn't to motivate.** "Great talent motivates itself." The converse of this means that if you have top-notch sales talent, part of your job as a CCO or compliance practitioner is "not to demotivate them". But more than simply not 'demotivating' your job should be to encourage "long-term commitment: sustained motivation over time."

7. **Talent needs to trust each other more than it needs to trust the manager.** This directly relates to the culture you set. If the only way for employees to succeed is to steal and cheat from their co-workers, you will have a toxic environment. Think of this in the context of your FCPA investigation protocol; if your goal is to skin some employee to save the company, you will not have much credibility left with your other employees.

8. **Improve the talent.** Unfortunately, most managers spend most of their time managing incompetent employees. The authors believe this is a wasted opportunity as most top talent "have a gift for learning and a desire to improve. That desire often drives their career choices." For a CCO this means you need to provide such opportunities to those on your compliance team. But think about taking this concept out into the workforce. What if you could offer a top sales person or executive a chance to not only learn something but

also advance their career by a rotation through the compliance department or a signature project they could lead?

9. **99% of recruitment is about who you don't sign**. Here the message is to use your background due diligence to make sure that that 'someone' is the right person in the right situation because "Introducing a weak or undisciplined player [employee] can damage the standards and culture."

10. **Accept that talent will eventually leave**. "Few talented people are looking for a job for life." Indeed in the compliance arena, since there are no trade secrets around anti-corruption compliance, the skills a compliance practitioner uses can be easily translated into another company. I often think about Jay Martin, the CCO of BHI, he is now on his third generation of compliance practitioners who work under him. While they are at BHI they have the chance to work under and for one of the top in-house compliance practitioners around and for a company that has a robust compliance program. They work very hard while they are at BHI but they get great experience, a great resume entry and a great reference from one of the top compliance practitioners around. If you are a CCO you might consider the BHI model.

11. **Gauge the moment when talent reaches its peak**. In the sports world, the only person who wins every time (eventually) is Father Time. While that may not be as true in the corporate world, burnout is true. I went through it in my 40s as a trial lawyer and many others do as well. If you are a CCO and see reduced enthusiasm or commitment in an employee this may be the reason. Would you consider a sabbatical for the employee? How about a plumb overseas role to rekindle the passion? As a leader, you need to recognize this issue and use your leadership skills to address the situation.

The authors note, "Talent management has been a business obsession at least since 1997, when the consultancy McKinsey identified a "war for talent."" As a CCO you should certainly consider these issues in managing your compliance function. However, I believe the concepts laid out by Forde and Kuper work for the broader corporate world as well. If you are going to use you influence throughout the organization, you should consider incorporating these techniques into your skill set.

7. Entrepreneurial Leadership in Compliance

Another area for CCO leadership influence can be found by looking at the skills need for entrepreneurial leadership. I came across such inspiration when reading an article entitled "*10 leadership skills for entrepreneurs*", by Gregg Swanson. While Swanson's piece was designed to help an entrepreneur understand "how to handle a demanding situation while leading others", I also found his ideas useful for the CCO.

A. **Assemble a committed team.** Even if you are a solo in compliance at your company, you will need a compliance team. If you have the resources to hire others, Swanson advocates for you to "Put an end to socializing methods and selling talent. Instead, focus on building a team that is committed and possess the skills to be successful." Regardless, every CCO works with a leadership team and others in the organization. You must get them committed to compliance.

B. **Communicate without limitations.** Here Swanson recognized that "Solid communication with other coworkers is essential, if the business wants to be successful. After all, if your team doesn't communicate, how can they know what is expected of them?" Certainly this is an important part of a CCO's role in dealing with others in the compliance function. However, I also think it can have much wider implications for the compliance practitioner. Communicating not only *what* is expected but also *how* and *why* compliance will help the business unit is critical to the success of any compliance officer.

C. **Make your business mission statement clear.** Swanson wrote, "An entrepreneur may assume clients and coworkers understand his or her objectives. In many cases, they probably do. As part of your approach to leadership, ensure that you revisit the mission statement with them to ensure that it's correctly understood." The same holds true for the CCO or compliance practitioner. You must make the compliance mission statement clear going forward.

D. **Reveal true genuine leadership.** For an entrepreneur, Swanson believed that "You'll never be that great leader simply by emulating the actions of others. But you can learn from the success and failures of others. Your employees are going to believe you more when you are dependable and real." This is true for the CCO or compliance practitioner, only 100 times greater. If you are sitting in the CCO chair on your way to bigger and better things in the corporate world, you will never be taken seriously as a compliance practitioner. Worse, your company's compliance program will not be taken seriously and the results will probably bear this out.

E. **Identify all of your barriers.** Swanson wrote, "Most entrepreneurs believe that they are working towards their ambitions and goals. There's nothing wrong with this. But a thoughtful leader will be the individual who takes the time to identify his or her own shortcomings." In compliance, there are always course corrections that need to be made. This is a basic premise of any *best practices* compliance program.

F. **Build a flexible team and provide them with the right direction.** It is critical when you are an entrepreneur trying to raise a successful team, to be "flexible with your team members as they define the function of things, influence the limitations or accomplishments they achieve." For the compliance practitioner, the agility to move and adapt is a critical component of not only your compliance program but also your personnel. This is true whether they are your direct reports in the compliance department or you are using others outside the compliance department to facilitate your compliance program.

G. **Put some trust in your team.** Swanson correctly noted, "In the business world, trust is essential. For the entrepreneur, there is a need to assist the growth of the group and to work past problematic periods. Strong leaders are people who others trust. Their assurance gives assurance to the group that everything will turn out fine." Once again this prong is only amplified in compliance. No CCO can micro-manage as there is simply too much to handle. You have to learn to trust your team going forward. Yet you can also depend on technology to help verify that trust.

H. **Acknowledge people's talent and give appropriate credit.** While it may seem self-evident, "One of the worst things you can do for your business is not to provide people with the credit they deserve. Many leaders can pull off an incredible presentation, but they always give credit to the people who helped them to shine." As a leader in compliance, you need to give out credit to not only those on your compliance team but also others in your organization who may further your compliance efforts going forward.

I. **Motivate your team.** As a lawyer who came into the compliance field, this was a concept I was not familiar with from my in-house experience. It is important to remind myself and perhaps others who may have begun in a corporate legal department that "You can't become a great leader if your workplace is dull and you have a team that doesn't care. You need to provide your team with moving demands. You can't generate a great deal if a team doesn't think based on their work."

J. **Expect the unexpected.** If there is one thing that all entrepreneurs should expect it is to expect the unexpected. Swanson said, "When you are an entrepreneur you need to have some kind of backup and safeguard in place that will help you to remain protected in extreme circumstances. With the current economic situation being incredibly harsh, it is important that you do what you can to avoid the pitfalls that can destroy a company." Nothing could be truer for a CCO or compliance practitioner. Yet by moving from reactive to preventative and then prescriptive, you can get ahead of the curve and be ready to respond, quickly and efficiently.

8. Finding Smart Risk in Compliance

Kathleen Finch, the Chief Programming Officer for HGTV, Food Network and the Travel Channel, was profiled in the article "*'Piling On' to Get Better Ideas*". She had some interesting ideas around the concept of "smart risk" and how you could use this concept to influence others.

Finch said, "One of my favorite things to do is to put a team together in an informal way, then figure out who can do what best. Not everybody likes that because I will oftentimes change somebody's responsibilities pretty significantly. But I like people playing to their strengths. Some of my best performers are people who had very different jobs than the ones they're doing now." This is one area CCOs do not usually consider approaching as an avenue for assistance. However I know of one company that brings in non-compliance specialists for rotation through the compliance function. But focusing on the strengths of such persons to aid in a compliance project might provide you with some added firepower going forward.

Finch continued this theme of using her team members' strengths, when she talked about another technique she uses which she calls "piling on" meetings. Bryant wrote, "I bring about 25 people into a room and go over all the different projects that are coming up in the next six months, and the goal is that everybody piles on with their ideas to make those projects as successful as they can be. The rule walking into the meeting is you must forget your job title... It is amazing what comes out of those meetings."

Think about this in the context of a roundtable or other form of corporate interaction where a CCO or compliance practitioner will try and solicit information about enhancements to a corporate compliance function. Finch said, "I don't want the marketing person just talking about marketing. I want everyone talking about what they would do to make this better."

Interestingly Finch used a term which I do not think is used enough in the business context, which she called "smart risk". She went on to say, "when things don't go right, I'll talk about what we learned from the mistakes. We celebrate our failures just about as strongly as we celebrate our successes because I need to encourage the team to keep coming up with the big ideas." It seems to me that she is expressing how to manage risk better and more intelligently, which certainly is an endeavor that every CCO needs to commit to doing going forward.

9. CCO as Colleague in the C-Suite?

This area of influence was explored by Adam Bryant when he profiled Margaret Keane, CEO of Synchrony Financial, in an article entitled *"When Hardship Informs Leadership"*. I found the article had some excellent influence factors for the CCO to consider in not only the role as a leader but also the role of a colleague to others in senior management.

When leading the compliance function or otherwise acting as a leader in any organization Keane pointed to the need to respect others in an organization. While many lawyers certainly do not take this into account in their role in a corporate legal department, it is a requirement in the compliance function. Keane said, "The biggest thing I learned when I first started managing people is that you really have to respect the people who were there before you showed up. So you could come in with all these great ideas, but if you come in acting like you know it all and you don't get the buy-in, then they will reject you."

Another key ingredient Keane talked about was how you interact with your subordinates, but not with the normal platitudes you associate with a CEO. She talked about working with talented and smart people under you. She said, "Another important lesson was getting comfortable with the idea of having people work for you who are smarter than you. When you're young, there's an insecurity that you have to do and know everything. There are leaders who never learn that lesson, even later on in life."

When it came to leading with your peers at the senior management level I found her next thoughts insightful. Keane believes, "A leader has to be decisive. The most frustrating thing for any organization is when you're just waffling around and no one knows what to do. You're going to make mistakes, but you're better off moving the organization forward than having them waffle. And then you have to be very clear with the organization about what's happening and why." Once again her remarks point out a clear distinction between the legal department and the compliance function. Many corporate legal departments are very good at presenting or at least explaining options. This is what lawyers do. However, this is not what the compliance function or CCO do. The role is to prevent, find and fix issues before they become problems or FCPA violations.

Keane also spoke about another angle to leadership not often discussed. It is the perception that she could not make difficult decisions. I found the reason and her response something a CCO often faces. Keane noted, "there was a perception that I couldn't make hard decisions. And the reason they thought I couldn't make hard decisions was because people liked me. I would get really angry about it because I know how to make hard decisions, but it's always about how you treat the process when you're making the hard decisions."

I found this point very perceptive. A CCO generally has to be liked to do their job. They often struggle with how well they will be perceived if they have to say "No". Keane makes clear that it is about the process. If you lay out your reasoning, having considered all the relevant facts, almost everyone will respect your decision because the process is rigorous.

Keane also talked about something that is becoming a greater problem as the compliance program matures and more compliance practitioners grow into the role of a CCO. She related, "because I've worked my way up, I know a lot of things. So it's easy for me to want to jump in and try to solve something. So I've learned to hold myself back from solving the problem and to let the organization solve it first."

Finally, Keane ended with three points that are useful for any employee, which I found to be particularly applicable to a CCO or compliance practitioner. First she said that you must "work hard. You're not going to get anywhere if you don't dig in and work hard. And that means doing things you don't like doing and not complaining about it." Second, she noted you need to ask questions. Moreover, if you are not getting enough from your boss or out of an assignment, then "raise your hand "to get some attention to have the situation clarified."" Finally, and perhaps most importantly, "pick your head up from your phone. Look around, see what's happening, engage socially. As much as we think they're social, they're not really that social because they do everything on their phones."

10. Being Nice and Compliance Leadership

Adam Bryant profiled Peter Miller, the CEO of Optinose, a pharmaceutical company, in an article entitled *"To Work Here, Win the 'Nice' Vote"*. Miller has some interesting leadership concepts that are applicable to the CCO and how to use influence to lead, not only in the compliance function but also across an organization. It was to be 'nice'.

You rarely hear this concept talked about much in the corporate world. Yet Miller learned this lesson about influence because as a "young sales manager at Procter & Gamble. I had five salespeople working for me, and one of the guys was 55 and another guy was 48. They were really successful salespeople, so I realized that I couldn't teach these guys anything about selling. Since I couldn't teach them anything, I tried to cultivate trust and respect by working really hard at figuring out how I could help them in a meaningful way."

This apparent inability to lead in precisely the area he was tasked in leading led Miller to formulate "a very important core value of mine, which is that you can and should try to create friends at your company." But more than simply becoming friends, Miller came to the understanding that underlying the friendship "is this concept of trust and respect. When you get that as a team, that's when great things happen. And that comes from creating a culture of openness, of authenticity, of being willing to have fearless conversations. It's about being yourself, not being afraid to say what's on your mind."

As a CCO, you need to be able to have that type of conversation with those both up and down your chain of command. Certainly it is always beneficial to have the type of relationship with your team that allows the full flow of communication. Miller said, "Think about how people are with their best friends. You want them to succeed. And sometimes that means having really hard conversations. If that's what's motivating you - and you're really trying to help everybody around you in a company as if they were great friends of yours - that's really powerful."

I was interested in Miller's insights in the managing up role. You have to be able to have some very frank conversations with your CEO and Board members about your compliance program and any issues that may arise under it. As CCO if you "cultivate trust and respect by working really hard at figuring out how I could help them in a meaningful way" as Miller used with his more senior sales team members, it should certainly help you going forward when you have to manage up your chain.

I also thought about this somewhat enlightened approach as contrasted with another style that I read about in a piece by Lucy Kellaway, entitled *"Wrong skillset excuse masks coup at the top of Barclays"*, where she discussed the recent termination of Antony Jenkins from Barclays Bank. The newly installed chairman of the company's Board, John McFarlane, who simultaneously promoted himself to

CEO, Jenkins former position, fired Jenkins. The reason Jenkins was fired; he no longer had the right "set of skills" for the organization. Chairman McFarlane explained to Kellaway that there were four skills going forward which (apparently) were lacking in Jenkins: "a) strategic vision; b) charisma; c) the ability to put plans in place that deliver shareholder value; and d) ability to ensure results were delivered." Ironically, Kellaway noted that lawyers for Kleiner Perkins had said that Ellen Pao "was an employee who never had a skillset."

Kellaway noted the obvious when she wrote "To invoke skillsets in hiring is not only ugly, but dangerous. Finding the right person to run a very big bank is very hard, and having a list of skills that you are matching an applicant against is not necessarily the best way of going about it." More ominously, she noted that the head of such bank would have to be able to rein in the traders and investment banker types who brought Barclays its unwanted regulatory scrutiny. More critically from the compliance perspective, I think it says much more about Chairman McFarlane that he did not say anything about a new CEO running the business ethically, in compliance or in any other manner which could help to prevent Barclays from another very large fine or penalty from the regulators.

McFarlane's dictum is one that will certainly be noted by regulators on both sides of the Atlantic going forward. After the disastrous run by former Barclays' head Bob Diamond, the bank was moving in the direction of regulatory compliance while securing the profits demanded by shareholders. However, McFarlane's sacking of Jenkins could well derail the bank's focus on ethics and compliance and engender the former attitude which led to the bank's fine in the LIBOR scandal.

Unlike Peter Miller at Optinose, it does not appear that Chairman McFarlane appreciates the trust and respect style of leadership. I fear things may well turn out badly for Barclay's yet again with the newly found emphasis on profits, profits, and profits.

PART IV - CONCLUSION

Effective Leadership, CCO 3.0 and Beyond

As the compliance function matures, the roles called upon by the CCO and compliance department teams will continue to both expand and grow. The worldwide explosions of corruption scandals, best exemplified by Volkswagen (VW), will put more pressure on corporate compliance functions to be prepared to respond to persons and groups as diverse as the Board of Directors to the CEO to regulators, shareholders and even the public. The skillset needed for this most important role will continue to grow as well.

As many compliance practitioners came out of a corporate legal department or have a law school background, they traditionally have received very little training on how to lead. Knowing the answer or going to look it up and they writing a well-crafted memo thereon was about as much leadership training as those persons received. However, in now the second half of this decade, those legal-training skills are simply not enough to be effective in the wide variety of roles a compliance practitioner currently has and will have in the future.

To be an effective compliance officer, you have to embrace skills that you may not have been trained for academically. These leadership skills are required to move compliance into the DNA of an organization, it will take much more than the brute force used by most corporate legal departments. Persuasion, influence, and communication skills will be required going forward. After all the roles of compliance and legal are very different. A corporate legal department is there to protect the interests of a company while the role of compliance is to prevent, find and fix problems before they become legal violations. Put another way, the role of legal is to tell the truth and the role of compliance is to tell the whole story. These are different roles that require very different skill sets in today's corporation.

Nonetheless there are specific skills, tools and techniques that you can use to move forward both the message of compliance and burning it into the fabric of your organization. I have laid out some of the tools that I believe you can implement at little to no cost to you and your organization. The role of the compliance function has moved from the structural change identified in Compliance 2.0, where the CCO function moved out from under the legal department to the a functional unit, to CCO 3.0 which advocates the incorporation cutting edge communication tools, for example social media, for the two-way discussion by the compliance function. Moreover, the workplace is evolving. As a leader, you will need to evolve your leadership skills to lead generations as diverse as the greatest generation, to baby-boomers, gen-Xers, millennials, and I-gens. Both soft skills and hard skills are needed.

Made in the USA
San Bernardino, CA
01 March 2016